Business Writing That Counts!™

Dr. Julie Miller

HARA
PUBLISHING GROUP

Published by
Hara Publishing
P.O. Box 19732
Seattle, WA 98109
(425) 775-7868

Library of Congress Cataloging-in-Publication Data

Miller, Julie Pascal 1947-
Business writing that counts!
Julie Pascal Miller - 2nd ed.

   p. cm
   Includes bibliography notes and index
   ISNB 1-883697-75-1
   1. Business writing   1. Title
   98-93336

Grateful acknowledgement is made for permission granted by
Pantheon Books for excerpts from *Bird by Bird* by Anne Lamont,
1994; and by the *Seattle Times*, 1986, 1998, 1999, 2000; permission
has also been requested from *Travel and Leisure* magazine.
Some graphics reproduced using ClickArt®ImagePack: 1996, 1997,
Broderbund Software, Inc. All rights reserved. Used by permission.

Manufactured in the United States
10 9 8 7 6 5 4 3 2

Editor: Vicki McCown
Cover Design: Eran Becker
Indexer: Judith Gibbs

Dedications

This book is dedicated:

To my extraordinary and ever-patient husband; his love and support sustain me.

To my dear and generous father, whose mentoring challenged and empowered me.

To my precious and beloved mother; she would have been so proud.

ACKNOWLEDGEMENTS

To Vicki McCown, my editor, a thousand thank-you's. Her love of words matches mine. With her wisdom, wit, and invaluable assistance, this book is a source of pride.

To Sheryn Hara, who navigated the difficult waters of the book publishing process.

To those I interviewed on writing, thank you for your honesty and for sharing your world of work with its writing frustrations and successes.

To my all clients, whose contributions continue to add to the depth and breadth of this book.

CONTENTS

INTRODUCTION

This millennium has been coined the "writing-est" of times... Words fly over the airwaves at the blink of an eye. With each new technology advance, the speed increases and so does the pressure. Customers demand instantaneous response; they want the answers and they want them now. If you can't deliver, you can bet that someone else will. Getting your message written and sent *quickly* is one issue. Making it interesting, clear, concise, and powerful is another. *Business Writing That Counts!* helps you with both.

Let's be honest. Writing tops very few people's "favorite" list. (Bright, hard-working people invent the most amazing excuses for not getting to it.) Writing is viewed by most people as difficult and frustrating work, and the consequences of ineffective communication are legendary. Poorly written documents create unnecessary waste—of time, money, energy. And the amount of lost revenue due to missed opportunities is inestimable.

The good news is that this book makes the writing process easier and less painful for you by teaching you a simple system to get it done quickly!

Business Writing That Counts! provides practical strategies for your work world. Whether you need to write newsletters, memos, or reports for large corporations, medium-sized companies, or home-based businesses, this book will help you *get organized, get started, and get writing.* The first three chapters set the foundation with a quick and easy brainstorming process, a unique numbering system, and the permission to break writing rules we were sworn to uphold. The last three help you refine your writing, address common business writing concerns, and present you with invaluable writing tips.

This book is designed for you to read sequentially, learning and building skills as you go.

But you can also pick it up and read any chapter of interest or concern. I have attempted to make this subject user-friendly and pragmatic. And as corny as it sounds, I also want you to feel empowered, to know that if you can talk, you can write!

Business Writing That Counts! has four main benefits for you, the reader. It will:

- Save you time which ultimately saves you money

- Increase your productivity

- Make your writing more interesting

- Provide you with a numbering system that you can apply no matter what you have to write

Turn the page and let's get started. And welcome to the world of quick, easy and powerful writing.

An important note to my readers: Good teaching involves using an effective and time-honored method: Review information for the learner, show examples and models, provide opportunities to practice the new skill, and then apply the new skill to a variety of tasks. So you will see throughout the book:

- Review

- Practice

- Apply

Here's to good writing!

PS: All quotes are referenced in back of book.

CHAPTER ONE

GET ORGANIZED

QUIT CIRCLING THE COMPUTER!

We all have to write, some of us on a daily basis: e-mails, faxes, memos, performance reviews, letters, business plans, proposals, reports, white papers . . . the list goes on. I say **have to** because it's the rare person who loves to sit down and put on paper what could be *told* to someone in half the time. I think novelist Gene Fowler best described how many of us feel when it comes to writing: "Writing is easy. All you have to do is sit down . . . and wait for drops of blood to form on your forehead."

> **"Writing is easy. All you have to do is sit down...and wait for drops of blood to form on your forehead."**

Instantaneous is just too darn slow!

With the advent of technology, writing is back in style. *And* writing on demand is a constant. But therein lies the rub! The ineffective writer has no place to hide! No longer are writing tasks delegated to the administrative assistant or secretarial pool down the hall. *Everyone* is expected to write. No longer is a client willing to wait a week for snail mail; the pressure's on to deliver and to deliver fast.

Thus, technology has become the albatross and the eagle. Though it allows us to soar, it also burdens us. While it simplifies and improves our work lives, it also complicates them exponentially. And with each new software iteration, the necessity for quicker feedback amplifies. This constant demand for immediacy raises the stakes *and* our blood pressure!

Disaster lies in wait if expediency replaces clarity. When you don't have enough time to spend on what you write, do you find yourself stuck with the following unwanted results?

❑ Missed opportunities because the writing team lacked efficient and effective skills

❑ Higher labor costs from rewriting unclear documents

❑ Damaged reputations because of poorly written documents

❑ Thinner bottom lines when proposals are rejected due to poor quality

Not spending time to make your writing clear, cogent, and concise may be hazardous to your career or to your business.

Writing eats up time

We also know *the time* that writing can take, gobbling it up like Pavarotti at a bake sale. The entire process generates huge amounts of fear, worry, and procrastination, usually involves criticism (by self and others), and takes a *great deal of time* to organize. A recent client of mine, the owner of a local placement service, told of his frustration in getting out a letter to his customers regarding a new billing procedure. He said, "Something's wrong with this picture. I just spent three hours writing three paragraphs that were read in three minutes! Not to mention the cost of mailing the darn things!"

So we circle the computer or, in my case, clean every nook and cranny in the office.

Why did it take him so long to write a brief letter? Because too much time was used on *the start-up*, meaning the organizing steps. He had no writing system in place that would help him quickly organize his thoughts and get the document out to his customers.

So we circle the computer, schmooze with coworkers, or, in my case, clean every nook and cranny in the office. *Anything to avoid getting started.* Why? Two reasons: We don't know where to begin, and we get hung up on following (*let alone remembering*) the sacred rules of writing.

Don't feel bad; you're not alone. A recent survey of over 1,000 professionals concluded that what bothered them the most when it came to writing was—you guessed it—getting organized and getting started.

A survey

I repeated the same survey locally, polling people in a variety of work settings: software developers, financial professionals, entrepreneurs, school superintendents, radio announcers, bankers, firefighters, police officers, retail store owners, stock brokers, administrative assistants, paralegals, military personnel, hospital administrators, and nonprofit directors.

> **Good writing is writing that works. It makes sense. It's both comfy and elegant. It says just enough and no more. It has manner, not mannerisms. Good writing has all the right words—and not too many of them—in all the right places.**
>
> **Patricia T. O'Connor**

The response was overwhelming. *Getting started* remained the single most difficult step for them in the writing process. A computer consultant told me she had no trouble thinking about what to write; it was the actual act of beginning the task that presented the most daunting hurdle. A local newspaper editor concurred. He confided that only after it became more painful not to start (translation: deadline) than to start, did he finally begin the task.

What stops you in your tracks?

Review the excuses below. Do any of these ring true for you?

- ❑ I'm so lousy at writing.

- ❑ It takes too much time.

- ❑ I never know what to say.

- ❑ I'm just not smart enough.

- ❑ I'm not *into* suffering.

- ❑ I *hate* having someone critique my writing.

- ❑ I'd rather *call* than write to my client.

- ❑ It's not my area of strength.

- ❑ I'm embarrassed to have anyone read my writing.

So enough already! You've admitted your frustrations and fears. Now, just shrug them off and jump right in! You'll enjoy the journey—I promise.

Business Writing That Counts! focuses on giving you better methods for getting your message out—to your customer, your supervisor, your colleague—and in *less time!*

In this first chapter, you will learn how to overcome the *getting started* hurdle and *quickly* organize your thoughts by using **Idea Maps**. You will also gain an additional benefit: *permission* to break some of the rules drilled into you in school.

For that reason, I will start by giving you immediate dispensation to get going and quit circling the computer! Or, as Davy Crockett said, "Root, hog, or die!"

RULE-BREAKER NUMBER ONE: THROW OUT THE FORMAL OUTLINE!

We've all had a teacher sometime during our school career who believed in strict adherence to the rules. Mine was Sister Mary John, a nun who had just come to America from a *cloistered* order in Poland to teach. Her *mission in life?* To cram into our pointy little heads *the writing rules*—rules for diagramming sentences, comma usage, dependent and independent clauses, prepositional phrases, nouns, verbs, *ad nauseam*. Sister would pace back and forth with the infamous yardstick and call out our names. If we forgot a rule, she would slam the ruler down on the nearest desk, muttering (we were sure she was swearing) under her breath in Polish. We lived in mortal fear that Sister would cast those penetrating, lashless blue eyes in our direction and demand answers!

Throw out what Sister Mary John told you about the outline rules.

Maybe you didn't have as colorful an experience as this one, but I'm sure you had a teacher who put the fear of God in you when it came to the writing rules. Following the rules and writing correctly reigned supreme—not making our writing interesting! The emphasis in school was on how to make our papers "correct."

One of the cardinal rules never to be violated was that *no idea* could be released onto the paper until the outline was written, reviewed, and returned. (*So we wrote the paper first and then did the outline.*)

Learning those important fundamentals gave us the basics. However, *fun* was not part of the drill-and-skill

The real issue, then, is knowing which rules you can break.

regimen. Those rules seemed designed to prove what was wrong with our writing rather than acting as powerful and positive tools to help us along the way. The lingering effect today is that these rules keep us from getting organized, getting started, and getting writing.

Who remembers the rules to outlining, anyway? We know it starts with Roman numeral I (one), followed by a capital A, then a cardinal number. After that, the structure becomes more fuzzy. Is the number supposed to be in parentheses or do we just use a period? Do we indent or not? Must we have three items or can we get away with less?

Who cares? These kinds of *nitpicky* questions are what make outlining a painful, laborious, frustrating, and totally unnecessary exercise. What you need is a simple system for getting your thoughts down, a system that does not layer a cumbersome process (e.g., the formal outline) onto your organizing efforts.

Spending most of your time on getting started is inefficient. No more than 25 percent of your allotted time should be relegated to the start-up, with the balance being spent on the revision and refinement of your document.

As you go through this book, you will learn how to write with competence, confidence, *and* speed. And best of all, you can thumb your nose at some of those rules!

IDEA MAPPING: A SIMPLE PROCESS

The easiest way to reduce your start-up time is by replacing the formal outline process with an Idea Map! What's that? An illustration of your ideas on any topic. Your thinking is displayed on paper similarly to how your brain works—in a nonlinear, multidimensional way. Various names for this practice, this visual tool include mind mapping, clustering, or webbing. I call it **Idea Mapping**.

If you pay too close attention to the rules of outlining, they will block the flow of your ideas and thus your words.

Idea Mapping can be applied to any kind of writing project and gives a structure to your ideas while helping you unlock your creative genius.

Whether you know the topic and just want a faster system for getting your ideas down, like the financial analyst organizing data on trends in the timber industry, or you need to generate new ideas, like the software company developing an employee compensation package, Idea Mapping can work.

Why? Because paying attention to the rules can literally stop you before you get started.

Why? Because formal outlining takes too much time and diverts your focus!

Why? Because your best ideas, your most creative ideas, come when you let go in an unedited, disorderly way of thinking.

Why? Because you want those incisive, creative ideas in your document.

Idea Maps work!

If: you already know your subject and want to see all your ideas on *one page*, the Idea Map *works*.

If: you are trying to brainstorm what you will actually write about, the Idea Map *works*.

Chart your own map

Whether you have to prepare projects, reports, proposals, RFPs, letters, even speeches, Idea Mapping provides a shortcut to simpler, more efficient organization.

Like brainstorming, Idea Mapping keeps you focused and allows you to ignore the internal *naysayers* as you generate your ideas. While providing structure, it keeps you focused. By staying *focused* you eliminate a time-waster—going back to organize your thoughts.

Before we go through the seven steps of Idea Mapping, let's look at two **example**s of a completed Idea Map.

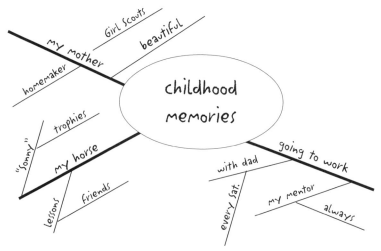

Example A: *An Idea Map of childhood memories for a family scrapbook*

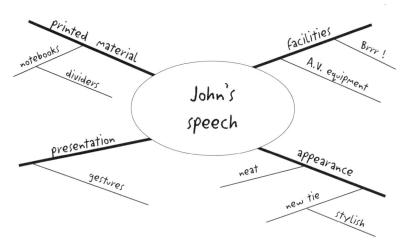

Example B: *A critique sheet of a speech used during John's debriefing*

Dr. Julie Tip: Idea Mapping can generate twice as many ideas as the conventional listing and outlining of topics. Why? Because according to the latest research, our brain does not necessarily process information in lists. Create Idea Maps and free your brain!

In the following pages, you will learn seven easy steps for organizing your ideas without being bogged down by the rule-laden formal outline process. No magic, just practical, visual guides. Once you practice these steps, in no time you'll be able to Idea Map a letter in *five minutes flat!*

 ## Review: The steps

 To get started you need a blank piece of paper and a pencil or pen. Your brainstormed ideas will be graphically displayed on the Idea Map.

Put down the main idea that you want to write about in the center of your paper. Use a single word or a phrase (abbreviations are fine) and draw a circle around it. (Figure 1) Since I've stressed the importance of saving time, the main idea in this **example** is *time management habits.*

Time
Management
Habits

Figure 1

 Dr. Julie Tip: An easel-size pad of paper or a white board is great for large group projects. Everyone can see it!

Next, consider these questions:

❑ *What is your purpose?* To persuade, explain, sell, apologize, inform, or entertain? Decide.

❑ *Who is your reader*?* What does he/she *need to* know (rather than what do *you* want to tell them)? Keep an image of your reader in your mind's eye. What does your reader feel or think about your topic?

❑ *What do you want your reader to do with the information?* Sue? Send money? Throw your message into the circular file? Call you?

I can't write without a reader. It's precisely like a kiss—you can't do it alone.
John Cheever

The reader remains at the heart of your writing. Unless you write to the reader, don't even pick up the pen, don't even put your fingers to the keyboard! The whole *purpose* of your document must be to engage the reader so that he/she does something with your information.

PS: The answers to these questions will focus your thinking and thus your mapping.

*Read more about the Reader in Chapter Three! Also, check out the Reader Meter in the Appendix.

Now, start filling in the Idea Map by answering this question: *What are the major points, the key concepts, important ideas of my main idea?* (See **example** of mapping question in next step.)

As your ideas come, keep your reader and the purpose of your document in the forefront of your brain.

 As you brainstorm your major points, draw lines out from the circled main idea. (Figure 2) Write down words and phrases rapidly on those lines (*no sentences—they slow you down*). Keep those freewheeling ideas coming. They can hitchhike on each other. One idea will trigger another and then another.

Don't make judgments as to whether the points completely fit with the topic. You will decide later which ideas you will use.

PS: Don't be concerned that this process seems random or chaotic or disorderly or messy or informal. It is all of these! Relax and just jot the ideas down anyway.

> **Our thinking processes have always yielded riches when we've approached things openly, letting free associations form into new ideas. Many would argue that we've used such a small part of our mental capacity because of our insistence on linear thinking.**
>
> **Margaret Wheatley**

On the lines radiating out from your circled main idea, you will fill in the *major* points, the key concepts about your main idea. Write down the words and phrases that answer the questions in Step #4 above. (Figure 2)

In this **example**, the important habits that help manage one's time are mapped.

Mapping Question: What would be important time management habits to practice?

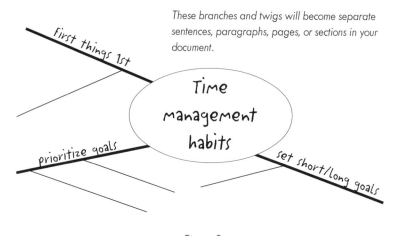

These branches and twigs will become separate sentences, paragraphs, pages, or sections in your document.

First things 1st

Time management habits

prioritize goals

set short/long goals

Figure 2

5

As you generate ideas that further support or detail your major points, start adding lines (twigs to your branches) with words or phrases. These become your minor points or details that add increasingly specific information to your major points. (Figure 3)

These instructions are presented in sequence. Your ideas will not necessarily come to you that way. You'll think of a major point or minor detail about one idea that will trigger an idea about something else. Perhaps some of your ideas may not seem to fit under any of the branches. Write them down anyway on the Idea Map.

Mapping Question: What data, examples, explanations, clarifications, or descriptions about your major points can you use to support the main idea? In this **example**, the minor points (twigs) list the specific ways you can acquire time management habits.

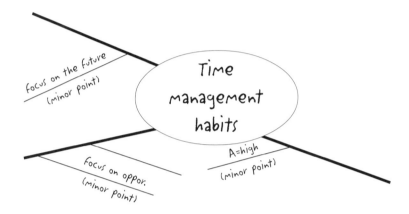

Figure 3

Continue to generate major points and minor details until you have finished. That may sound like a silly statement, but you'll know when you're done. (Allot at least five minutes.) Either you'll run out of ideas, or the data that you gathered will have been placed on your Idea Map, or you will be clear on what you want to write.

Blocked? Can't think of anything? Just draw some lines radiating out from your main idea. With this simple act, you will release the mental logjam in your brain. Why? Because your brain cannot stand incompleteness and it will eventually think of a word to put on those lines. Amazing, huh?

When you're finished, step back from your Idea Map. Become a critical thinker. **Decide what major points will stay and which ones will go.** Determine what minor points can be combined or deleted or actually belong under another point.

Then, circle the individual big branches with the major and minor points on them. This will make it easy for you to see the number of points you plan to make in your report, letter, speech, or proposal. (Figure 4)

Last, determine the order in which you will write your document. Then prioritize your ideas by placing a number next to each circled branch. (Figure 4)

Later on in this chapter, I'll show you additional ways to organize information.

A completed (and circled) Idea Map

Figure 4

In this Idea Map, you will find:

❑ key concepts (habits) about time management

❑ abbreviated words and phrases

❑ major and minor points

 Even with a major report that requires lots of data, you can still (with practice) complete an Idea Map in ten minutes.

Dr. Julie Tip:

For group writing projects:
Circle each major point with different colors to make them easier to see. Then assign each branch to individual team members. Each team member Idea Maps their branch and adds further data or information necessary to the project. This works great for business plans, grant or proposal writing— actually any large document!

Idea Maps at work:

💡 A large engineering firm in Seattle planned to expand their consulting services to include environmental engineering. This expansion involved setting up new departments, adding personnel, and developing a separate division within the corporation. Using the Idea Mapping techniques, they mapped out all work to be done by quarter's end. Additionally, they drafted the contents of a new company brochure.

💡 A computer consultant to one of the largest auto dealerships in Washington uses Idea Mapping when he attends any training or continuing education class. "It's so fast! I can take all my notes on one large 11- by 14-inch piece of paper. Sometimes I take an even larger pad with me for multiday training."

💡 A dean of students at a private college said procrastination used to be her middle name when it came to completing requests for recommendation letters. These requests would all come at once at the end of the school year. She wrote, "After drawing up an Idea Map on a Sunday afternoon, I felt much better about taking on this daunting and time-consuming chore!"

Idea Maps save you time!

Here's the dean's Idea Map. She made a template, or a model, to use for all her letters. This same template could be used for performance appraisals/reviews.

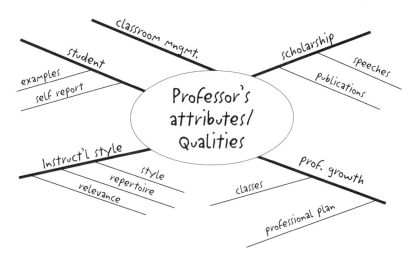

examples
student
classroom mngmt.
self report
scholarship
speeches
publications

Professor's attributes/ Qualities

Instruct'l style
style
repertoire
relevance
classes
prof. growth
professional plan

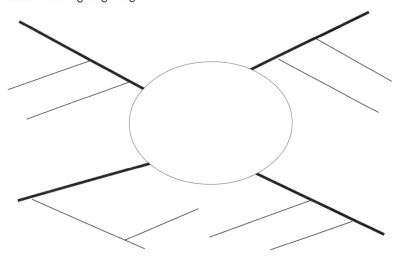

Practice: Now you try it

Apply the steps and create an Idea Map on any topic, perhaps an idea for a family vacation, a speech on a marketing proposal, a response to a customer complaint, or a plan for a product roll-out. Try several to practice. After charting six or seven Idea Maps, you should be able to create them effortlessly. To start, put your main idea in the center of the map below and get going!

Four More Ways to Idea Map

Information can be organized graphically in many different ways. Depending on your writing tasks—letters, proposals, reports, marketing materials, speeches, projects—perhaps one of these Idea Map formats will work for you.

Four additional ways to organize your thoughts, data, or points into an Idea Map follow:

1. Division of information

2. Comparison and contrast

3. Cause and effect

4. Problem and solution

But *remember*: No matter what format you use, it must be reader-oriented. Ask yourself, how will I effectively and concisely present my points to the reader? (See Reader Meter in the Appendix) **Examples and questions** to help you use the different formats are presented below.

1 Division of Information

Dividing information remains probably the most widely used organizational format because of its built-in natural logic. You can organize the information in one of the following ways:

- Chronological
- Most to least important
- Least to most important
- Listing of steps

As you Idea Map, consider these Mapping Questions:
- ❑ What will occur first, next, last?
- ❑ What major problems need to be addressed?
- ❑ What steps should be followed, chronologically or by degree of importance, in this process?
- ❑ What reasons, from most important to least important, should be considered for supporting this project?
- ❑ What seem to be logical divisions for the presentation of this report/proposal?

Scenario: The beginning marketing plan for a new product for ABC Corporation.

Mapping Question: What key areas should be considered as we take this product to market?

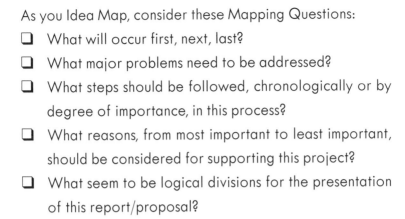

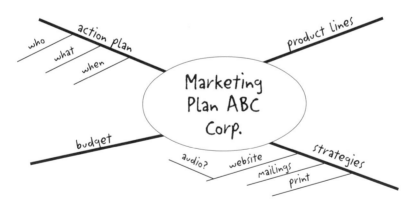

2 Comparison and Contrast

In this next format, you can organize data by contrasting and comparing and/or presenting advantages and disadvantages. For **example**, perhaps you want to compare the attributes of your product/services versus that of your competitor.

As you Idea Map, consider these Mapping Questions:

❑ How can I use familiar ideas to link to unfamiliar information?

❑ How will I compare and/or contrast our product/service to that of our competitors?

❑ In what order do I approach the advantages and disadvantages of starting this project?

Scenario: A discussion by a hospital's board of directors about whether to use public or private monies to fund prostrate cancer research.

Mapping Question: What are the major considerations regarding public versus private funding?

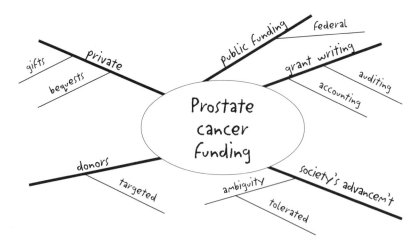

3   Cause and Effect

You can also organize your information around a question-answer or cause-and-effect format, which means you consider what effect could result from a certain cause. For **example**: If we proceed this way, this will happen; if we proceed that way, that will happen.

As you Idea Map, consider these Mapping Questions:

❑ Should I analyze the information from simple to complex ideas or sequentially?

❑ What will be the effects of this decision?

A cause-effect example: Uninteresting and poorly written marketing material is difficult to read, which can lead to disinterest, anger, frustration by the reader, which leads to...No sale! which leads to...No job! which leads to...

Scenario: A fast-growing software company considering the causes and effects of using in-house trainers versus contracting with vendors.

Mapping Question: What would be the cause-and-effect relationships between in-house training versus outsourcing?

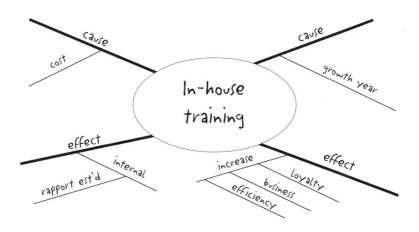

4 | Problem and Solution

This last approach has universal appeal. People learn from observing how others solve problems. For **example**: Here's a problem and here's how we solved it, *and* with these results.

As you Idea Map, consider these Mapping Questions:

- ❑ What facts, reasoning, and conclusions are needed to reach a decision?
- ❑ What data and anecdotes can I use to drive home the solution to my reader's problem?

A problem-solution example:

Problem: 90 percent of all head injuries could be prevented if people wore bike safety-helmets.

Solution: An aggressive ad campaign that includes giving bike helmets to the local elementary school.

Scenario: Limited parking is available for employees. The problem becomes compounded by the fact that this business shares the same entrance with a local community college.

Mapping Question: What might be some solutions to the problem of not enough parking?

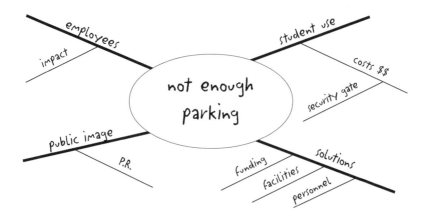

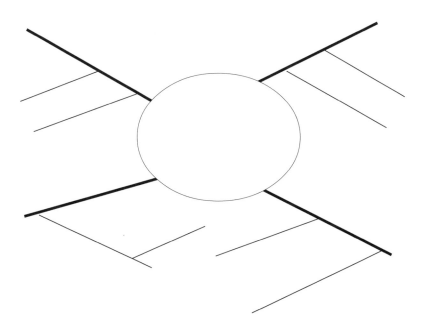 *Apply: You're on your own*

Now it's time for you to chart your own Idea Map. Use existing documents or create additional documents to help you get started. For **example**, how about Idea Mapping the business plan that needs updating or the series of instructions necessary to create a database? Try one of the Idea Map formats (see pages 20-24) and map a current project.

 Important: Hold on to your Idea Map, and in the next chapter, you'll use it to get writing!

Idea Mapping can help in other ways:

- 💡 **Preplanning**: Idea Mapping organizes major projects and reports. It allows for brainstorming and creativity *before* you begin the work.

- 💡 **Test preparation**: Idea Mapping organizes lecture notes or chapters in a text that you are studying. It makes it easier to see all the important points on one piece of paper.

A colleague of mine used Idea Mapping to study for the comprehensive exams in her doctoral program. She said, "There was absolutely no conceivable way to study four years' worth of material by using a formal outline. The outline would have been as thick as our course notebooks! Idea Mapping was the only way. We could see an entire course on one very big piece of butcher paper. Our study groups worked off those Idea Maps and we all passed!"

- 💡 **Note-taking at meetings or lectures**: Idea Mapping simplifies getting down the main points covered. Even when a speaker *bird walks* (goes off on a tangent— see definition at end of chapter), you can still capture the ideas on one piece of paper without critiquing the speaker's organizational skills.

- 💡 **Problem solving**: Idea Mapping gives you permission to think through an issue creatively.

The theme running through this entire book is how to save time while producing clear and effective writing that gets read. The Idea Map will *save you time*—guaranteed! Your end of the bargain? To practice the steps so that they come easily to you. When given a document of any length to write, you can quit circling the computer, get organized, and get started.

In Chapter Two you will learn how to turn your Idea Map into powerful writing by using numbers. The numbers will keep your writing on target and cut your time in half!

You may want to put a place holder here for easy reference.

Singing from the same songbook

Each of the following words and definitions will help as you go through this book. Having a common vocabulary is important, as you may not be familiar with some of the words. In other cases, you may have a different interpretation.

Bird walk	Going off on a tangent; important information that needs to be included but may be slightly off course; an aside.
Concluding Power 1	Sentence or paragraph that seals your document. See Chapter Three.
Free-writing	Getting your thoughts written down without regard to the formal rules of writing. Using your Power Outline or Idea Map as a guide. See Chapter Two.
Idea Map	A graphic representation of your ideas on paper.
Mnemonics	A memory technique. See C.I.E.V.R. Solutions in Chapter Four.
Pedantic writing	Writing that no one understands but may impress some.

Power numbering	An organizational writing system that assigns a numerical value (a power) to words, phrases, sentences, and paragraphs.
Power 1	The main idea of your document. It can be used at the beginning and end of a document.
Power 2	The major point(s) about your topic. It explains or supports your main idea. Power 2 always talks about Power 1.
Power 3	A minor point or detail about Power 2. Power 3 always talks about, supports, elaborates on Power 2. Power 4's and 5's can add even further specifics. Just remember, each power must make some reference to the preceding power.
Power Outline	Organization of your Power Numbers and ideas.
Transitions	Words, phrases, or sentences that link your ideas.
Voice	Revealing who you are through your writing; your unique way of expressing yourself.
Zero Power	Sentences that hook the reader.

IN SUMMARY

Using Idea Maps will:

✔ Help you quickly generate ideas or organize data

✔ Free you from the fear and procrastination of getting started

✔ Open up your creativity without the mind-numbing outline structure

✔ Provide an organizational tool when you already know the topic

✔ Allow you to see your entire writing project at a glance

✔ Provide an excellent process for group projects or large reports

✔ Help make sense of large amounts of data

✔ Organize one-page letters or 1,000-page tomes

What's Next?

In the next chapter, you will:

- Organize your Idea Map into a Power Outline

- Master the Power Numbers system

- Understand how using the Power Numbers helps you produce clear, crisp communication

- Convert the Power Outline into a draft with Power Sentences

- Practice free-writing that first draft

Moving right along...

Chapter Two

Get Started

Cut Your Writing Time in Half!

Now that you have completed your Idea Map, let's get started by using the **Power Numbers** system. I tell my clients, "If you can count to three, you can write anything you ever have to in this or any other lifetime!" This is not a false claim. Read on.

I have taught the Power Numbers system—a process elegant in its simplicity—to over 110,000 people in every imaginable industry: from school districts to software conglomerates to insurance companies; from professionals to service people to students; from CEO's of large corporations to small business owners to one-person enterprises; to government employees, hospital administrators, restaurateurs, travel agents, realtors, attorneys, financial planners, and accountants, just to name a few!

> **If you can count to three, you can write anything you ever have to in this or any other lifetime!**

Everywhere I have taken this system, positive results have occurred! People feel empowered, successful, and confident. They say, "This is so easy! Why didn't I learn this in school? I wouldn't have been so afraid to write." Another frequent comment: "I can't believe how much time this saves! I can easily organize my ideas with this system!"

A dirty little secret

I'm going to let you in on a little secret: all expository writing—whether informative, research-based, persuasive, technical or analytical—follows a formula. The writer introduces the main point of his/her document then proceeds to logically unpack the ideas. For **example:** *Here's the idea, here are major points about it and here are some specifics to back it up.* In turn, the reader looks for that clear organization and the details, the evidence of support.

The trouble comes from the fact that in school we were taught abstract terms that English teachers loved—topic sentence/thesis statement, introduction, body and conclusion. They may have meant something, but in most cases they did not contain clear images that helped us write a clear and cogent paper. Thankfully, the Power Numbers system shows you how to logically unpack your ideas to get the results you want. The numbers provide a concrete strategy to *getting started* and *getting writing*.

Use numbers to write

This simple system uses numbers to give order to your thinking and your writing. It quickly organizes your ideas into a logical sequence without the rigid rules of formal outlining.

THE POWER NUMBERS SYSTEM

A quick explanation of the Power Numbers (below) will help you get started. This system consists of assigning a numerical value (a Power) to words, phrases, sentences, and paragraphs. The numbers correspond to the level of importance and detail you want **This is so easy! Why haven't I learned it until now?** in your document. *The Power Numbers stay the same whether they represent words, phrases, sentences, or paragraphs.* By using the numbers, you can quickly organize your ideas and get writing!

To explain:

1 2 3

Numbers are your friends!

❏ **Power 1** is the main idea, topic sentence, topic paragraph, thesis statement, big idea, or focus of your document. It may be the first sentence of your document or be included within the first paragraph. Power 1 can also be used as a concluding sentence, restating your main idea, topic sentence, or big idea. (More details in Chapter Three)

❏ **Power 2** is a major point or detail about your Power 1. It clarifies, explains, or supports your main idea. Power 2 always talks about Power 1. Power 2's make up the body of your document.

❑ **Power 3** is a minor point or detail about Power 2. Power 3 always talks about, elaborates upon, or adds specific details about the major points (Power 2's). Add as many Power 3's as you need to back up your major points.

PS: You can add increasing levels of detail to any document of any length. How? By adding **Power 4**'s and **Power 5**'s. In most documents, you will only need Power 2's and 3's to make your point; in others—depending on the purpose—more detail is necessary. Just remember, each number must support or relate to the preceding Power Number. To see models of this expansion, look for **Advanced Examples** in the Appendix.

Also, for those of you who think in pictures, here's another way of seeing this whole system extended out to Power 4's and 5's.

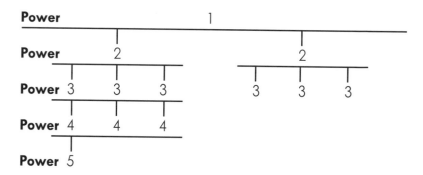

Now let's get back to business

We've discussed what the big picture looks like. Now I'm going to pull apart a paragraph and show you just how expository writers logically unpack their ideas. You can do the same. Use the numbers to organize your writing and thinking.

Here's a simple paragraph with each sentence defined as a Power 1, 2, or 3.

Follow these three steps to turning on your computer. (Power 1) First, be sure you plug it in. (Power 2) Purchase a power-surge cord to insure against future problems. (Power 3) Second, press in the button on your PC tower. (Power 2) You will hear a whirring sound; this is the computer starting. (Power 3) Last, press the button on your monitor. (Power 2) Your monitor will spring to life with color and graphics! (Power 3)

The Power 1 states the topic; the Power 2's support the main idea; the Power 3's provide the details.

Start with Power 1's and Power 2's

Use the numbers to organize your writing and thinking. A short **Power Outline example** about favorite European cities using Power 1 and 2 words and phrases follows.

The Power 1 is favorite European cities (the main idea) and the Power 2's are the names of the cities (the major points).

Power 1=favorite European cities
Power 2=Positano
Power 2=Dalkey
Power 2=Cambridge

How about this example:

Power 1=international airlines
Power 2=British Air
Power 2=TWA
Power 2=Northwest Airlines

And here's one more:

Power 1=financial institutions

Power 2=Bank of America

Power 2=Key Bank

Power 2=Cascade Bank

Power 2=Wells Fargo

 Practice: Now you try it

Working with **Power 1**'s and **Power 2**'s, complete the following Power Outlines below. How many major points (Power 2's) will clarify or explain the program to your employees? To your customers? List your Power 2 ideas in the spaces below.

1 New customer service program

    2 _____

    2 _____

    2 _____   **List the major**

    2 _____   **components of**

    2 _____   **this program.**

Or perhaps you need to get out a memo informing your staff about a change in the organization. What three reasons would you share with staff?

1 Changes in the sales department

2 _____

2 _____

2 _____

Add Power 3's

Now, let's continue to flesh out your document. To add further information, you need Power 3's. Here the Power 3's add information about the European cities. The Power 3's list the countries where these cities are located.

Example:

Power 1=favorite European cities

Power 2=Positano

Power 3=Italy

Power 2=Dalkey

Power 3=Ireland

Power 2=Cambridge

Power 3=England

What specific points would you use to elaborate on the new customer service program or the reasons why changes have occurred in the sales department? Those examples would be your Power 3's. **Add as many Power 3's as needed** to explain, describe, define, illustrate, support your Power 2's.

 Dr. Julie Tip: You can add as many Power 2's and 3's as you want to make any point of any length.

Take your Power 2 points and write Power 3's for the following outlines: **You fill in the rest!**

---

1 New customer service program
    2 Increase customer loyalty
        3 For example, greet each customer
    2 Feel free to make decisions
        3 Specifically, may not need to check with
          supervisor
        3 _____
  2 _____
  2 _____
    3 _____

 Some Power 2's require additional elaboration; others do not.

Build the Power Outline

---

1 Changes in the sales department
    2 Mary, manager of the technical division, is (You fill in
      the blank!) _____
  2 _____
    3 _____
    3 _____
  2 _____
    3 _____

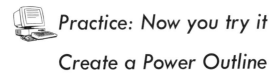

Practice: Now you try it
Create a Power Outline

Use existing documents or ones you need to write. Take the points covered in a meeting you attended this past week, a letter you received needing a response, a policy change that requires explaining, or perhaps your obligatory weekly report. Translate those points into a **Power Outline**. Use these simple template **examples** to organize your thoughts:

1 Weekly meeting
  2 _____
  2 _____
    3 _____
  2 _____
  2 _____

OR

1 Response letter
  2 _____
    3 _____
    3 _____
  2 _____
  2 _____

The Power Numbers system works because:

❑ The Power Numbers are concrete and logical. These numbers organize your thinking, your writing, even your speaking.

❑ With the Power Numbers, you control your writing by using however many Power Numbers you need to make the points you want. You don't get locked into following any prescribed outline format that slows you down and takes time. Your writing organizes around what makes sense.

Use Power Numbers to clear up these problems:

❑ **Organization:** The numbers make it easy for the reader to follow your thoughts.

❑ **Sequencing:** The numbers point the way.

❑ **Supporting details, examples, or anecdotes:** The Power 3's help make your case.

❑ **Gaps in information:** Ask yourself: Do the details (Power 3's) directly relate to what was stated in Power 2? Do the Power 2's really unpack the idea from your Power 1 sentence? Check to see.

AN EXPANDED POWER OUTLINE

The Power Outline can expand to any length—you decide. Just remember it is always based on your reader and the purpose.

Remember the Idea Map on *time management habits* in Chapter One? Here it is again. This time I'm showing you how the branches and twigs equate to the Power Numbers.

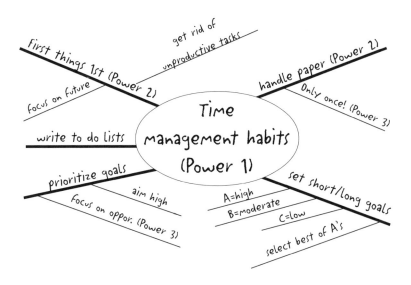

Here is the Idea Map converted into a Power Outline (See page 11 for the Idea Mapping steps):

 Throughout this outline, the Power 2's (major points) do not all have the same number of Power 3's (minor points) supporting them. In this system, you do not need the same number of details for every major point. However, the more support you have, the stronger the point. You decide; just consider your reader!

Power 1= time management habits
    Power 2= first things first
        Power 3= get rid of unproductive tasks
        Power 3= focus on future
    Power 2= prioritize goals
        Power 3=focus on opportunity
        Power 3=aim high
    Power 2= write to do lists   —— **This Power 2 has no**
    Power 2= set short/long goals   **Power 3's to support**
        Power 3= A= high   **it. That can work; it**
         depends on what you
        Power 3= B= moderate   **want to emphasize or**
        Power 3= C= low   **elaborate upon.**
        Power 3= select best
    Power 2=handle paper
        Power 3= only once!
Power 1= make time work

You did not see this Power 1 as a separate branch on the Idea Map as it is merely a restatement, conclusion, or summary of the Power 1. More details on this in Chapter Three.

The Power Numbers stay the same whether they are used to represent words, phrases, sentences, or paragraphs. Stay tuned and watch them grow and fill out into a full-fledged newsletter article.

PS: The entire process from Power Outline to newsletter article can be found in the Appendix.

 *Practice: Now you try it*

Power Quizzes

Identify the organizational structure by determining the *Power* (*1*, *2*, or *3*) in these paragraphs. Underline or highlight your answers in the paragraph. (Answers in Appendix)

> | **1** | "There are *two* Seattle's on prime-time television. One is rendered by *Millennium*,
>
> the Friday-night creep show…The result is a depressing hour of tele-
>
> **The transition words— one…the other—serve to guide the reader.**
>
> vision…The other Seattle of TV Land is a damned site more cheerful. *Frasier*, the hit sitcom on NBC, is ensconced in a stunning, immaculate Queen Anne apartment overlooking the Space Needle and downtown."
>
> *Pacific Northwest Magazine*
>
> **Your answers:** __ __ __ __ __

2 "Egypt offers *six* advantages to American investment. It has a unique location with access to European, African, and Arab markets. It has the broadest industrial base in the Arab world. It has a large cadre of industrially skilled workers. It has a system of advanced vocational education centers that offer training custom-made to an investor's labor needs. It has investment laws that provide profit and capital repatriation privileges, and even more special advantages for firms operating in free zones. It has an eagerness to acquire and apply Western technology.

No obvious transition words (like those in the example above) are used in this paragraph. But you can easily follow the six points by the writer's repetitive use of the words *It has.*

Nation's Business

Your answers: __ __ __ __ __ __ __

3 To others, the whirlwind of activity seems more like a new variation on Mark Twain's Gilded Age, a time of reckless speculation and profiteering. Amid the hubbub of buying and selling, a host of probing questions are being asked about the stock market and its relationship to U.S. capitalism in general. Has the market become more volatile, risky and perhaps more irrational than ever before? Is it suddenly too treacherous for the ordinary investor? Is the very function of the market changing, as fast-buck artists crowd in to pursue big, quick returns that have little or nothing to do with industry or commerce? Have the values of the gambling hall undermined the role of stock trading as a means of productive, long-term investment?

This is a much subtler example than the others. The author asks the "probing questions" (Power 2's) of the reader about the stock market mentioned in the Power 1.

Time magazine

Your answers: __ __ __ __ __ __

Here's a more sophisticated **example** with Power 4's and 5's. If you would like a challenge, see if you can chart the Power Numbers. If not, continue on and come back later.

 The common currency of Europe is a godsend to U.S. citizens, who are enjoying the euro's short-term price advantages and long-term conveniences.

First, the short-term advantages: The value of the euro has slumped about 11 percent since January. That means that people who are exchanging dollars are getting all goods and services in Europe—from bus rides to restaurant bills—for 11 percent less than they would have paid in January.

In addition, the euro has dropped close to parity with the dollar—one euro equal to $1. So close, in fact, that the euro serves as a sort of instant foreign-exchange calculator. Prices are often quoted in the local currency and the euro. All a U. S. visitor has to do is look at the euro price to determine the price in dollars.

The writer's clear use of transitions—first, in addition—courteously guide the reader.

Long term? In 2002, the euro will start circulating paper bills and coins, eliminating costly and confusing conversions from dollars to franc to lira to marks.

The Seattle Times

Your answers: __ __ __ __ __ __ __ __ __

PS: Again, if you would like to test your skill on **Advanced Examples,** go to the Appendix.

Some powerful short stories

One of the great joys in my work occurs when clients share success stories about how the Power Numbers system has worked for them. An assistant director of a large county agency told me "Precision is a nonnegotiable" in her office. "Mistakes in communication cost millions of government dollars. Using the Power Numbers to organize our complicated policy and procedure manuals was a lifesaver! The manuals were just plain simpler to read."

A nationally recognized college debate team used the Power Numbers in an unusual and clever way. Having sat in on my class, they told me that the Power Numbers could be used to organize their required tournament impromptu speeches. The Power 2 points were their fingers; the Power 3 details were their knuckles! No one would guess why the debaters' gestures were so powerful! "Using the Power Numbers kept us focused and organized."

A local United Way director said, "Learning the Power Numbers was easy. I have a logical mind, so the numbers just made sense. It's an informal outline approach that makes getting to my writing that much more efficient."

A different response came from my friend, a radio and TV announcer in California who does the financial news. "I tend to be very global and random in my thinking process. So, my speaking can sometimes be all over the map. The Power Numbers help me stay organized in this incredibly warp-speed job. I use the numbers to clarify issues for my listeners. For **example:** the three key points in the new tax law; or the five important ideas that Greenspan stated in his last pronouncement; or the one essential component to 'playing the market.'"

A highly regarded software company that creates programs for graphic artists uses the numbering system with its development team. "The numbers guide the conceptual flow for our products. This is the key we were missing!"

Nowhere is reducing writing time more crucial than in the tech world. Software start-ups are on the fast

No *turtle-footing* allowed!

track, running at double time. The tasks of finding initial funding, putting up a website, and getting product to market push these companies to move at breakneck speed. "The numbering system gave us the framework for writing our business plan, the web text, even the product descriptions. We saved money because we saved time!"

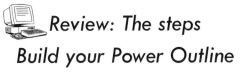

Review: The steps
Build your Power Outline

Take out the Idea Map you created in Chapter One and convert it into a Power Outline as I did with the time management topic. Organize it according to the Power Numbers. Get the words or phrases down. You'll convert them to sentences a little later.

Follow these steps.

Write down the main idea (from your Idea Map) of your document. The circled word or phrase in the middle of the Idea Map represents the Power 1.

Count each branch (the lines radiating from the circles). That number determines the number of Power 2's, the major points you will write about. In my Idea Map, I have five branches; therefore, five Power 2's list the time management habits.

 Count each twig off the main branches. Those represent the Power 3's—the minor points about the topic.

 Build your Power Outline using the words and phrases from the Idea Map.

This section introduced a second fail-proof method to help you get organized and get started: the Power Numbers system.

In the next section you'll take your Power Outline and turn it into clear, crisp, concise memos, e-mails, letters, reports, proposals—anything you need to write. By using the Power Numbers system, you save time. Knowing how many points you will write about in your document cuts your organizing and writing time **in half**. And you will deliver **writing worth reading**.

Let's Get Writing and Start Counting!

Congratulations! You've made it over the first hurdles: You've organized—charted an Idea Map (or two). You've started—used the Power Numbers to Power Outline your topic. Now, you can begin writing directly from your Idea Map or your Power Outline.

Writing that first sentence!

At this point, you don't want to waste time trying to construct a glorious opening sentence. Simple is best. You'll come back later and revise. Use the following strategy to get writing!

1 **Count the number of Power 2's from your Power Outline <u>or</u> the number of branches on your Idea Map**. That total will determine how many points you will write about. For **example**, you might have *four* components to the new customer service program or *three* reasons for changes in the sales department.

PS: You will save your readers time with this device. They can skim your paper by reading just the major points.

2 **Write that number in your Power 1 sentence**. Why? Because using a number in the Power I sentence quickly gives you an organizational mind-set, and permission to just start writing. You know where you're going, you know how many points you're going to write about and guess what—so does the reader!

A birdwalk: Putting a number in the Power 1 sentence is not an absolute! But it jump-starts your writing. I'll show you other ways in Chapter Three to put your Power 1 sentence together. Stay tuned!

Once again, looking at the *time management* **example,** the Power 1 sentence from the Power Outline could read: Your passbook to a rich and full life will be assured if you practice these *five* indispensable time management habits.

Now, for your first draft, write your Power 1 sentence from your own Power Outline:

_____

_____

Here are other examples of Power 1 sentences using a number to guide the reader:

1) Three charming cities in Europe should not be missed!

2) Our new customer service plan offers five money-saving ideas.

3) Due to product sales decline, our sales department must undergo three personnel changes.

4) In this era of expanding education rhetoric but restrained state spending, it's useful to compare two ideas. (*The Seattle Times*).

5) Contemporary politics has three peculiarities. (*The Washington Post*)

6) Two e-mail improvements are most welcome! (*The Seattle Times*)

Free-Write, but With Restraint

Does that sound like an oxymoron? Free-writing conjures up images of blithely dumping down on paper whatever darn thing comes to mind, then spending excessive amounts of time going back to organize those chaotic thoughts.

But with the Power Numbers system, you can free-write and organize at the same time. Here's how: As you let those ideas flow freely, use the Power Numbers to capture them, thus creating some semblance of order **while saving time!**

Worry-free free-writing

Your internal editor may be itching to use his red pen, but tell him to keep a cap on it for now. Just get your words down without much attention to punctuation, spelling, the rules. By using your Power Outline or Idea Map you exercise a bit of control so that you stay focused and don't wander. The Idea Map or Power Outline acts as a guide so that less time will be spent later reorganizing the material.

> **Never correct or rewrite until the whole thing is down. Rewrite in process is usually found to be an excuse for not going on.**
> **John Steinbeck**

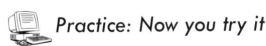 ## Practice: Now you try it

Take your Idea Map or Power Outline and begin your draft. For guidance, you can refer to the draft of my *time management* article or go to the Appendix .

Dr. Julie Tips:

For beginning this draft:

- Use whatever writing tool works for you. Some people can compose directly on the computer, others find writing in longhand more comfortable.
- Start with whatever section seems easiest for you. You could start with the body of the document, next work on the introduction, and then write the conclusion.
- Tell yourself that no one will read this first draft.
- Tell yourself that, although writing is a necessary and sometimes daunting chore, you'll get through it.
- Give yourself a time limit, approximately twenty minutes, to just free-write. Take a break, and then come back and re-read what you wrote. It will help you get started again. But do not spend time "correcting" *yet*.
- Recognize that this first draft is tough, messy, and undisciplined; still, just let go and free-write. Mastering this technique remains important.

Remember, a first draft is just that—a first attempt. A necessary exercise, it enables you to produce a great final piece of writing. It's like building a house: You need to lay the foundation first to have something to build upon.

Rewriting is where you should spend your very valuable (and in short supply!) time. Similar to putting a jigsaw puzzle together, the fun lies in seeing the pieces fall into place. The parts become whole and form a clear picture, the one intended by the designer. (More on the rewriting process in Chapter Three.)

Everyone writes that dreaded first draft...

...even good writers! Author Anne Lamott, in *Bird by Bird*, described her writing of first drafts: "I'd write a first draft that was maybe twice as long as it should be, with a self-indulgent and boring beginning, stupefying descriptions...lots of quotes from my black-humored friends...and no ending to speak of. The whole thing would be so long and incoherent and hideous that for the rest of the day I'd obsess about getting creamed by a car before I could write a decent second draft."

Prolific author Peter DeVries confessed, "I love being a writer. What I can't stand is the paperwork!" In a more serious vein, James Michener was often quoted as saying that he wasn't a great writer, but the world's best re-writer. Another writer stated: "Like many writers, I don't like to write; I like to have written."

So, the value to you in this process? From your draft will come your final masterpiece!

Apply: You're on your own
Free-writing

In a couple of pages, you're going to get your draft down by free-writing. Here are two ways to approach the process.

Just free-write your Power 1 and 2 sentences and then go back and add **Approach this process** your Power 3's. **as if you were writing the *Cliff Notes* version of your final product.**

Add the Power 3's as you go. Add as many as you need to provide support, elaboration, expansion, or further development of your major points.

...perfectionism will ruin your writing, blocking inventiveness and playfulness and life force (these words we are allowed to use in California). Perfectionism means that you try desperately not to leave so much mess to clean up.
Anne Lamott

Do not let the internal (or infernal) writing police, armed with red pencils, hover over your shoulder and carp about every word and sentence you write. Trying to rewrite each phrase or sen- tence now will only block the flow of your ideas, slow you down, and waste time!

At this point, do not allow perfectionism to creep in.

On page 58, take your Idea Map or Power Outline and start putting down your sentences on paper. Work your way around the Idea Map or down the Power Outline. Use the Power Numbers as your guide.

As you free-write, some important bird walks:

❑ Know that the writing process is not necessarily sequential. You may choose to add your Power 3 sentences as you free-write and not in the sequence that I have described.

❑ Know that you can prioritize your points now or later. You can use one of the Idea Map formats to help with this.

❑ Know that you will revise your writing later—adding gestures (punctuation) that you would use as if you were speaking. (Now, if you're Italian, like I am, you may gesture much differently than if you're Irish.)

❑ Know that you can guide your readers by using transitions and keep them interested through sentence variety or word choice.

❑ Know that you can show emphasis by using different font styles or sizes, italics, bold, underlined words. Your choice will be based on your reader.

❑ Know that you reveal who you are through your writing. You have your own unique way of expressing yourself. Your style—your voice—needs to come through in your writing.

❑ Know that you will add words that create pictures. Using vivid language creates certain images depending on your audience. For instance, you would choose different words for NRA members than you might for the Bartenders Association.

 Know that you need to quickly engage and connect with your reader through these choices.

Continue working on your draft here:

1 _____

    2 _____

        3 _____

        3 _____

    2 _____

        3 _____

        3 _____

TIME MANAGEMENT HABITS OUTLINE CONVERTED INTO SENTENCES

Here are Power 1 and 2 sentences from the Power Outline (from Chapter One) on the five *time management habits*. Remember they are just in draft form!

A Draft

Example:

Power 1=Practicing five indispensable habits is your passbook to a full and rich life.

Power 2=Do first things first.

Power 2=Prioritizing your goals is the second habit.

Power 2=A third habit consists of writing to do lists.

Power 2=Set short- and long-term goals.

Power 2=Learning how to handle the slew of paper that arrives each day is important.

Power 1=Make time work.

The Power Numbers stay the same whether they represent words, phrases, sentences, or paragraphs in an Idea Map, Power Outline, or final product. Stay tuned and watch them grow and fill out into a full-fledged newsletter article. For a graphic illustration, go to the Appendix.

Power Paragraphs

Here the sentences have been reworked and expanded to form paragraphs. Thus, the whole of the paragraph pertains to that Power. Power 2 and 3 sentences are combined into one paragraph and, where appropriate, Power 3 paragraphs stand alone in order to flesh out the document.

As you know, paragraphs usually only contain one main idea. So the Power 1 paragraph states the main idea, the topic of the article. The subsequent paragraphs (Power 2 paragraphs) discuss each point, in this case, the five habits.

Your passbook to a rich and full life will be assured if you practice these five indispensable time management habits.

— **This is a Power 1 paragraph—it states the topic. See Chapter Three for tips on writing introductory paragraphs.**

Start by focusing on first things first. By determining the most significant work for you to accomplish, you narrow your concentration to a few activities that get results. Since not enough time is available to do everything, choose the most significant tasks and pour your energy into those.

Power 2 paragraph describes the first habit.

Second, prioritize your goals. Your goals must be centered around opportunities rather than past failures. Only through ranking your objectives will you achieve focus.

Power 2 paragraph describes the second habit.

A third habit consists of writing to do lists. Goal-oriented people always write things down. By doing so, goals become more

Power 2 paragraph describes the third habit.

than just ideas. Writing makes them real.

Fourth, setting short- and long-range goals should become an — **Power 2 paragraph describes the fourth habit.**
ingrained habit. This process consists of deciding what level of importance each of them has. Then organize the tasks around completing your goals.

Last, learning how to handle the slew of paper that ar- — **Power 2 paragraph describes the fifth habit.**
rives each day is imperative. Touching the same piece of paper more than once wastes an inordinate amount of time.

Making time work for you remains the most —— **A Power 1 sentence concludes the article. See Chapter Three for techniques on writing concluding paragraphs.**
important habit you *can acquire in today's extraordinarily busy world.*

 ## *Practice: Now you try it*

Sentences into paragraphs

Expand the *time management* article with Power 3 paragraphs. Just as the whole of the Power 2 paragraph supports the Power 1 (the main idea) in your document, so do the Power 3 paragraphs support the Power 2's by adding specifics, data, or perhaps rationale.

Here the Power 3 paragraphs expand the *time management* habits **example**. The Power 3 phrases were converted into sentences and then combined into a Power 3 paragraph.

 Where appropriate, each Power 3 (from the Power Outline) could become an individual paragraph—depending on the amount of information necessary to cover the topic.

Expanded Time Management Article

Your passbook to a rich and full life will be assured if you practice these five indispensable time management habits.

Start by focusing on first things first. By determining the most significant work for you to accomplish, you narrow your concentration to a few activities that get results. Since not enough time is available to do everything, choose the most significant tasks and pour your energy into those.

Repeating this daily mantra—I must do first things first—forces you to hone in on important work and eliminate those tasks that don't move you forward. — **Power 3 paragraph clarifies what it means to do first things first.**

Second, prioritize your goals. They must be centered around opportunities rather than past failures. Only through ranking your objectives will you achieve focus.

Focusing on future opportunities should drive the organization. You can't change what's happened, you can only prepare for what will happen. That's where your energy and attention must be directed—outward towards success. Remember to always aim high! — **Power 3 paragraph describes focusing on opportunities.**

A third habit consists of writing to do lists. Goal-oriented people always write things down. By doing so, goals become more than just ideas. Writing makes them real, concrete, and attainable. — **No Power 3 paragraph was needed here.**

Fourth, setting short- and long-range goals should become an ingrained habit. This process consists of deciding what level of importance each of them has. Then organize your tasks around completing the goals.

Power 3 paragraph gives you tips for labeling tasks.

Label these tasks A, B, and C. A tasks always get picked as they will create results. Those tasks labeled B are placed in a file that says "pending," while the C tasks are put in a drawer that may read "when hell freezes over." Translation: No time or energy should be spent on C tasks.

Last, learning how to handle the slew of paper that arrives each day is imperative. Touching the same piece of paper more than once wastes an inordinate amount of time.

It would stagger the imagination to consider how many times you handle a piece of paper before you act on it. Force yourself to make a decision about each piece of correspondence as it crosses your desk the first time. Will you file it, toss it, or respond to it? Choose. — **Power 3 paragraph details paper handling.**

Anyone can acquire these five habits. Simple, tested, and proven in the real world of work, they help you accomplish more—in less time, thus freeing up time for enjoyable pursuits. Making time work for you remains the most important habit you can acquire in today's extraordinarily busy world. — **Expanded paragraph= concluding Power 1 paragraph.**

1 2 3

Now, check your draft—

Count backwards!

If you read these paragraphs in reverse, you find that the Power 3 paragraph supports the major point contained in the subsequent Power 2 paragraph. The Power 2 paragraphs speak to the Power 1.

Go back up to the Power Numbers in your draft and check whether your sentences follow a logical sequence. This becomes your assurance that you stayed focused and organized.

Practice: Now you try it

Edit your document

Check over your paragraphs. Do you have:

- ❏ Power 3's that really talk about the preceding Power 2?
- ❏ Power 2's that unpack the main idea presented in the Power 1?
- ❏ An organizational structure appropriate for the audience?
- ❏ A document that accomplishes what you want?
- ❏ Enough information for your reader?

In Summary

The Power Numbers system works because it:

✔ Gets you started

✔ Gives you a shortcut

✔ Saves you time

✔ Helps you organize

✔ Results in lean writing; lean writing gets read!

✔ Stops you from circling the computer

✔ Helps you produce more powerful documents

All expository writing follows a basic organizational structure. Information is logically presented to the reader, then supported and defended through additional argumentation, recommendations, or data.

The reader looks for that structure. If the reader has to work too hard, you have erred in your ways. Use the numbers to keep your writing simple, direct, and well-organized.

In Chapter Two you learned how to organize your writing logically through the use of numbers. These numbers not only keep you and the reader on track but can also cut your writing time in half. Chapter Three presents the final step in the writing process: the rewriting and refining of your draft. This is where you must spend the majority of your writing time.

WHAT'S NEXT?

In the next chapter, you will:

📌 Understand how transitions smooth out style

📌 Break another rule

📌 Realize the importance of writing like you talk

📌 Review, revise, refine, rewrite your draft

📌 Learn how much fun this process is

📌 Practice writing beginnings and endings

📌 Learn Dr. Julie's Guiding Principles

📌 Produce a document worth reading

📌 Know how to use peer feedback *correctly*

Now comes the fun part!

Chapter Three

Get It Done

Rewrite Quickly and Painlessly

All good writers rework their words. When Ernest Hemingway was asked by George Plimpton, who was working for the *Paris Review* at the time, about the process of rewriting, the great writer confessed, "I rewrote the ending of *A Farewell To Arms*, the last page of it, thirty-nine times before I was satisfied." Plimpton probed, "Were there some technical problems there? What was it that had stumped you?" Hemingway's reply: "Getting the words right."

> **Approach revision with the same openness to inspiration with which you began writing the first draft.**
> **Dana Gioia**

Getting the words right

Getting the words right means taking a cold, hard look at your writing, trading the free-wheeling fedora you've worn up to this point for the critic's cap, and calling up those internal writing police to sharpen their red pencils.

Why? Because you need to adopt the attitude that this part of the writing process is the fun part! Does it involve work? Sure, I'd be lying if I said it didn't. But it's in the revising and rewriting that your imaginative problem-solving skills come into play. You get to scratch your head, step back, and think about how you can clearly and effectively communicate your message to your reader. And, with practice, you will gain both speed and skill.

So, a pause before you begin your rewrite...

Or as Tom said pointlessly, "My pencil is dull."

That's just what you want—a dull pencil—so that you will be forced to stop, step back, and get time and distance from your draft before you start sharpening your words. As author E.B. White advised in the *New Yorker* magazine, "Let the body heat go out" of your writing.

On the following pages, you'll take your draft and refine it. You'll work on style by getting the words right so that your message gets read. You'll see how transitions guide the reader through your document. You'll learn the importance of openings and closings. But most noteworthy, you'll find this process relatively quick and painless—*if* you paid attention to Chapters One and Two! So, as you begin your rewrite, review:

Dr. Julie's five guiding principles

1 Allow an hour or two away from your first draft; overnight is even better, assuming your boss doesn't want it by the close of business today! You will come back with fresh eyes and ears and really be able to see "where the shoe pinches."

> **Truly, I've seldom seen a piece of prose, a poem—my own or anyone else's—that couldn't be improved upon if it were left alone for a time.**
>
> **Raymond Carver**

2 Always read your writing out loud. You may read with your eyes, but you hear your writing through your ears. You will get a much better idea of the cadence, the inflection, the rhythm, where it makes sense, where a question mark goes off in your head.

3 Remember the "so what?" factor. Visualize your readers with those words tattooed on their forehead as you write. So what do they care? So what do they understand? So what should they do with your message?

4 Set aside time to write, especially if you are knee-deep in a project. Make an appointment with yourself, preferably at the same time each day. Turn off the phones, the coworkers, or any other distractions. You'll be surprised how much you can get done in thirty minutes, let alone an hour.

5 Run don't walk to the nearest bookstore or computer screen and purchase these essential books. These "must-haves" ought to sit at your work station:

❑ *The Elements of Style*, William Strunk, Jr. and E.B.White. The ultimate authorities on style. If you want to make sure you're absolutely correct, a more in-depth stylebook might be the answer. Consider *The Gregg Reference Manual*, *The Chicago Manual of Style*, or *The MLA Style Manual and Guide to Scholarly Publishing*.

> **No passion in the world is equal to the passion to alter someone else's draft.**
> **H.G. Wells**

❑ *Webster's Collegiate Dictionary*. No little wimpy paperback, but a real thick book.

❑ *Roget's International Thesaurus*. Get the big one with tabs. Do not rely on any software program to give you the depth and breadth of words that this book can deliver.

Dr. Julie Tip: If you're looking for pithy or memorable sayings to add to your document, check out some of the websites that list quotes. They usually are found under the search word *memorable quotes*. They could be used in a sales letter or brochure, even an executive summary or speech.

 ## Let's focus

Take your draft and give it the *litmus test* below. Then focus *only* on the areas that need reworking.

Answer yes or no to these questions: Yes   No

Does my writing accomplish my purpose?   ____ ____
Does it say *enough*?   ____ ____
Is it clear?   ____ ____
Are my ideas sequenced so that the
    reader can easily follow them?   ____ ____
Have I engaged the reader?   ____ ____
Will what I want to have happen,
    happen because of my writing?   ____ ____

In other words, have you clearly stated what you want from the reader? *Use your time and energy only on the no's.*

Remember Rule-Breaker Number One: Throw Out the Formal Outline? Well, before we continue, I need to give you permission to break another one:

> **A writer's best friend
> is the wastepaper
> basket.**
> **Isaac Singer**

 # RULE-BREAKER NUMBER TWO: WRITE LIKE YOU TALK!

I know your teachers said that writing was a completely different language than speaking, but they were WRONG! Your writing needs to sound like a conversation you would have with your reader.

I know that, in the world of business, writing is expected to be professional. But professional does not mean writing in a formal, stiff style or in a manner that will not help make the connection with your reader.

> No conscientious writer should complain of the trouble. Writing is a social act: whoever claims his neighbor's attention by writing is duty-bound to take the trouble—and in any case, what is life for, unless to do at least some right things?
>
> **Jacques Barzun**

Imagine explaining a process, describing a new product, conducting a personnel evaluation, or reviewing the year-end report.

See yourself sitting at your desk, standing in the conference room with your peers or even talking on the phone with a client.

You would speak in a normal, logically sequenced, conversational manner, using the appropriate language and voice for your audience. You would establish rapport, showing who you are.

That's the voice you want to project in your writing. Your writing should sound like conversation, only better, because you wouldn't have "uhs" or "ums" or use slang. Let your personality show through.

Technical writing

Even in technical writing, where you are allowed less latitude in how you present the material, you can define terms, present examples, include anything necessary to make your writing easier to understand. Though the tone stays professional and objective, the writing still needs to be readable. Or don't you care if they read your report?

Even government agencies understand the necessity of putting their words in more user-friendly language. Mike Billips of the *Atlanta Business Chronicle* noted that the SEC (Securities and Exchange Commission) has voted that "the use of stilted and legalistic writing shall cease." All stock and mutual fund prospectuses must now be written in everyday language, attorneys are being asked to use plain English, banks are rewriting their annual reports so that their stockholders can read them more easily, and city councils are decreeing that clear, understandable communication become the new standard. Not writing in plain English has gotten cities and municipalities in hot water. For **example**, poorly written initiatives have been misunderstood and citizens erroneously have voted down bills that would have increased state funding!

> **The reader's understanding of the topic is directly proportional to your understanding of reader.**

Consider your reader

In Chapter One, I asked you to keep your reader in your mind's eye so that your words strike the right note. Focus your writing on what the reader must know to make a decision.

Keep your ego out of your writing. The goal remains to *express* information rather than impress the reader. Remember the definition of an egotist: "one who is me-deep in conversation." Think about these points as you rework your draft.

❑ **Knowledge level**: What does the reader already know about the topic? Does the reader understand and enjoy reading words and phrases such as "heuristics," "interoperable intermodal transport systems," "paradigmatic analysis"? Or would the reader prefer a simpler style?

❑ **Format**: What type of document is required? A letter, proposal, RFP, e-mail? Your answer will determine how you format the text.

❑ **Personality**: What kind does the reader have? Does the reader prefer facts with ample data or an informal tone?

WRITE LIKE YOU TALK

It remains your responsibility to get your points across, to define the issues concisely, to help the people who read your writing understand. So write like you speak: simple, direct sentences, crisp explanations, clear images, ordinary words with a professional but personal touch.

How do you speak with your colleagues? Do you ask them about the "feasibility of creating a structure from indigenous vegetation"? Or do you talk about planting a tree to get some shade in the park?

Let's be clear. I'm not talking about chatting up the reader—that's not appropriate. I'm suggesting that you avoid a pedantic (highfalutin', flashy, affected, stilted) style that turns your reader off and wastes time. Take a look at the following **Simple Guide to Plain Talk.**

PS: I deliberately used the word "pedantic" to make a point! Note that my tongue is firmly planted in my cheek.

A Simple Guide to Plain Talk

Pedantic	Readable
ascertain	find out
aforementioned	these
as a result of	because
at this point in time	now
before long	soon
cease	stop
commence	start, begin
compensate	pay
correspondence	letter
demonstrate	show
desire	want
due to the fact	because
during the time that	while
elect	choose
facilitate	ease/help
for the purpose of	to
give consideration to	consider
implement	do
in close proximity	near
in the future	soon
in the event that	if
indebtedness	debt
indicate	show
in view of the fact that	since
locate	find
numerous	many
on condition that	provided
prior to	before
purchase	buy
rapid	fast
reason is because	reason is
residence	address
subsequent to	after
subsequently	later
sufficient	enough
terminate	end
utilize	use
vehicle	car/tool

> **The greatest barrier to change is the myth that clarity has to be sacrificed for precision, especially with complex subjects. Don't believe it. The murkiness that plagues so much official and legal prose...comes more from bad style than the inherent difficulty of the subject.**
> **Joseph Kimble**

Mark Twain makes the point about unnecessary verbosity quite eloquently: "I never write 'metropolis' for seven cents when I can get the same price for 'city.'" Syndicated columnist James J. Kilpatrick asked his readers: "What is the purpose of writing anyhow? ... It seems to me, it is not to enlarge our readers' vocabularies but to communicate an idea from the mind of the writer to the mind of the reader." So *write like you talk.*

What's write? What's wrong?

You judge! Look at these **examples** of pedantic writing.

An e-mail sent to a design team:

Team,

Per an e-mail from Mary last week informing me of the decision to delay the conversion of DXM into RLM, and in order to gain optimum utilization of the by-products of our refining activities, we can simultaneously achieve economic advantage from our selling activities if we utilize the sizing solution.

 Do you even have a clue what this says?

An opening description on the home page of a well-known software company's website:

(Company name) is endeavorily* determined to promote constant attention on current procedures of transacting business focusing emphasis on innovative ways to better, if not supersede, the expectations of quality!

***not a word in *my* dictionary!**

 How would you write it? What would be your response if this were sent to you?

And this direct mail piece:

Dear Consumer:

NaturallyTalking is the world's first large vocabulary continuous speech recognition system. With parsing you can achieve up to 99% accuracy rate. When we parse your words, we take between ten and fifteen megabytes of information.

 And this one? I think we might be left scratching our collective consumer heads.

PS: If you want to see the ultimate **example** of pretentious and pedantic writing, check out William Lutz's *Doublespeak*.

Dr. Julie Tips:

If you find it difficult to write like you talk, try these ideas:
- Imagine a friend sitting across from you. Start talking about your topic.
- Talk into a tape recorder.
- Call a friend and actually talk through your topic; then write it down just as you said it.
- Use simple words.
- Use contractions.
- Use personal pronouns like: I, me, my, our, you, your, we, us.

 When you use contractions, consider the reader, your purpose, and the accepted practices of your organization. Always determine their appropriateness.

 Practice: Now you try it

Rewrite these pedantic, verbose phrases (Answers in the Appendix.)

Pedantic	Rewritten
Please be advised that…	Please consider
Reference is made to your letter…	
Pursuant to your instructions…	
The question as to whether…	
Answer in the affirmative. . .	
For the reason that. . .	
In the near future. . .	

Apply: You're on your own

Now go to your draft. Eliminate any language that won't connect *you* with the reader.

ADDING TRANSITIONS

Let's continue to refine your writing by adding words that link ideas and make it easy for the reader to follow your line of thinking.

A **transition** is a word, a phrase, a sentence that helps the reader to see how your ideas connect. Transition words guide (or signal) your reader. They link your ideas together.

Transition words move the topic forward. They smooth out style, tell the reader what's coming next, or remind the reader what occurred.

French writer Anatole France said that writing is like carpentry and like carpentry "...you must join your sentences smoothly."

Words like…

first	second	however	next
finally	therefore	another	in addition
besides	for example	moreover	furthermore

…are commonly used to help the reader. (See the Appendix for a complete list.)

Always use the simplest transition devices you can and never overuse them. Otherwise, your writing will sound stilted, stylized, or patronizing.

The **example** below of transition overkill shows how overuse can insult or irritate the reader!

> People have always wanted to fly. *However*, until 1903 it remained merely a dream. *For example*, it was believed that human beings should not fly. *Specifically*, they were not birds. *Nevertheless*, the Wright brothers launched the world's first flying machine. *Consequently*, flying today in an airplane is part of our daily lives.

 If the writer had eliminated even two of the above transitions, the reader would have been a much happier camper. Just read it aloud and you'll see! Also, poor use of transitions creates boring sentence structure! Note that every sentence above is subject-verb.

Here's an example that works:

> Where's the economy headed, anyway? *First* it was the Goldilocks economy—not too hot and not too cold. *Then* the bears came home and Goldilocks was in trouble. *Now* it seems Goldilocks is settling down to a nice bowl of bear stew.
>
> *The Seattle Times*

And another one:

How has the president failed to ensure that the laws be faithfully executed? *First,* he has intentionally given false testimony before judicial bodies where he had taken a solemn oath before God and court to tell the truth and nothing but the truth. *Second,* he was at the very core of a conspiracy to obstruct justice.

The Seattle Times

 ## *Practice: Now you try it*

Add transitions to your draft. Refer to the list of transition words in the Appendix and try some out. Get a sense of which ones work or sound appropriate. You'll know.

Tricky Transitions

Another method of transitioning between ideas consists of using what I call **Tricky Transitions**. In the hands of a skilled writer, they prove very effective.

Tricky Transitions can be used three different ways:

 Repetition of a word or phrase from one sentence to the next.

Examples of repetition of a word or phrase:

Seattle's dazzling, well-loved school superintendent died yesterday morning. A community is grieving. [John] Stanford gave us leadership unseen in this town for years. He gave us strength through his stunning, positive attitude. He gave us a new sense of the possibilities of public schools, the heart and soul of this and any city. He could have gone off to a leisurely, monied, sunset career. Instead, he gave himself to the city's children.

The word *gave* **repeats.**

The Seattle Times

In Texas, US West and another regional Bell Company asked a federal judge to strike down a key provision of the Telecommunications Act.

In Washington State, US West tried to remove a critical regulatory power.

The word *in* **is repeated.**

The Seattle Times

Reference to an idea or a phrase from the previous sentence or paragraph.

An **example** of bringing an idea along:

Two other e-mail improvements are most welcome: First is the addition of signatures that can be tacked on to the end of every e-mail note and give a particular flair to one's electronic correspondence. These signatures can be utilitarian, such as one's name, address, phone number, etc. They also can be a favorite saying. Among my favorite signatures from notes I have received have been, "Bigamy: having too many husbands. Monogamy: having too many husbands."

The word *signatures* is repeated in the second and fourth sentence. The third sentence uses *they* to refer to the topic of the paragraph: e-mail signatures.

 Use of pronouns (he, she, it, etc.). The pronouns refer to ideas or people previously mentioned.

Here's a quick **example**:

From the moment [John] Stanford arrived in September, it was clear he'd never be a caretaker or a status-quo manager. He was a change agent...He was the two-star Army general who talked unabashedly about loving children.

Repetition of the pronoun *he*.

The Seattle Times

 *Practice: Now you try it*

Note the transitions. And just for fun see if you can determine the Power structure of this memo.

Memo

To: City Council members

From: Jason Brown, President, Chamber of Commerce

Re: Renaming streets

Date: February 18, XXXX

I was surprised to read in the *Woodway Weekly* about the city council's decision to change the street names as it creates considerable hardship for the entire business community. First, renaming the streets could cause a loss of revenue for business owners. New street names will only confuse customers trying to locate us. Second, renaming the streets forces us to spend unnecessarily. All our marketing materials—from stationery to cards to billing to brochures—will have to be redone. I find this totally unacceptable! Last, renaming the streets appears to be change for change's sake. Since the founding of this city, we have always had numbered streets. What's the hidden agenda here?

In this memo, Mr. Brown repeats the word *renaming* as his transitional device. It certainly drives the point home to the reader.

(Power structure: 1 2 3 2 3 3 2 3 1)

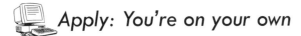 **Apply: You're on your own**

Go through your draft and see where you could add a Tricky Transition. Now check your draft. Do you have:

✔ Sentences that relate to each other by supporting the Power 1 idea?

✔ Smooth transitions that guide the reader?

✔ An organizational structure appropriate for the audience?

✔ A document that accomplishes what you want?

✔ Enough information for your reader?

Make it whole

Chapter Two let you in on the secret that good expository writers have always known (perhaps even intuitively). They understand how to unpack the information for the reader in a clear, logical sequence by making certain some reference is made to the preceding sentence.

But for the rest of us writers, the Power Numbers are heaven-sent because they concretely show how to build a document by organizing your ideas step-by-step, sentence-by-sentence, and paragraph-by-paragraph.

In this section I want to show you how to put it all together by viewing your document as a whole. Instead of scrutinizing each sentence to determine its Power, step back and view the paragraph as a whole unit. All the sentences combine to make the paragraph one collective Power Number.

We know that most documents are divided into three requisite sections—the beginning, the body, and the ending. The Power Numbers again come to the rescue! Look at the paragraphed *time management* article. The beginning or introduction is the Power 1 paragraph, the Power 2 paragraphs make up the body, and the last Power 1 paragraph represents the ending or conclusion.

Yes, even though individual paragraphs contain Power 2, 3, 4, or 5 sentences, the entirety of the paragraph represents one of the Power ideas. For **example**, the *whole* of the Power Paragraph 2 discusses the first habit, while the *whole* of the Power Paragraph 3 describes how to acquire it.

Let's now look at these three separate parts.

BEGINNINGS
Hook your readers

George Will, well-known historian, author, and intellectual, said that in this sound-bite society, "Survival is for the briefest." Being brief while engaging the reader remains even more crucial and twice as tricky in writing. You have about five seconds to capture your reader's attention. So, think sound bites.

And with writing for the World Wide Web, this is even truer. Key words and phrases must grab hold of the reader immediately. In this world of information overload, your writing has to stand out from the crowd. Those first sentences count!

However, each type of document requires a slightly different approach. Some need a beginning that captures interest right away; others may be more effective if they begin with a personal note .

Always know the purpose of your document as you rework

the beginning/introduction. That purpose will determine how you begin, how you will introduce the topic.

Ask yourself, is your document:
- ❑ a sales letter?
- ❑ a response to a query or complaint?
- ❑ a follow-up letter?
- ❑ the beginning of an annual report or brochure?
- ❑ an abstract?
- ❑ a cover letter for a job application?

Suggestions for great beginnings

Eliminate tired and hackneyed openings such as:
- ❑ Per your request
- ❑ Enclosed please find
- ❑ Please plan to attend
- ❑ Please be advised that
- ❑ Regarding our recent conversation

Your first sentences count! These phrases don't grip the reader. Instead, try making your openings more specific. **For example**, try these:

You requested information about...

or

I have enclosed the information that we discussed...

Build rapport with your reader right away.
You want your words to be meaningful to the reader. Starting off by saying:

We at Emcorp are taking strides to harness the power of the Web...

doesn't excite, unless you can show a benefit. But by adding,

...*so that you can gain competitive advantage*

would get the reader to sit up.

Consider this reader-focused benefit in an Avis mailer. I bet you'll open the brochure with these words on the cover!

Avis is trying harder for Mileage Plan members with a free day! for you.

3 **Use the word *you/your* within the first two sentences,** which creates a bond between you and the reader.

This came with my phone bill:

Dear Valued Customer:

Loyalty seems to be a rare commodity these days, particularly when it comes to long distance phone companies. That's why we're pleased by your continued...

Here's an **example** from a small-business newsletter:

Have you ever had a great idea, an idea so powerful you knew it couldn't miss, but you were unable to find the money to launch your idea? Frustrating, isn't it?

Nothing is wrong with starting off by thanking your reader. Just try to add something personal and specific:

Thank you for sharing the market research with us this week! Your efforts will surely help in securing our second round of financing.

 Use Zero Power sentences!

Zero Power Sentences

Zero Power sentences get the reader's attention. This technique of hooking your reader is used all the time in speaking. (Remember using startling statistics, fascinating facts, jokes, quotes, and certain words to engage the listener as you began your speech?) In writing, Zero Power sentences can be used the same way.

❑ Zero power sentences ask a question:
Can the tax code be cut to a paragraph?

❑ Zero Power sentences state a startling statistic or fascinating fact:
Chances are greater that you will be run over by a car in your neighborhood than die in a plane crash.

❑ Zero Power sentences alert the reader to important information contained in the document:
You've just won the car of your dreams!   Read on for the details.

❑ Zero Power sentences can begin with an incident, illustration, or anecdote:
I toured the city last night in the back of a police car. The close relationship between juvenile delinquency and lack of recreational facilities for teenagers hit me square between the eyes.

❑ Zero Power sentences can begin with a quote:
Thomas Edison's definition for genius has often been quoted: "Genius is one percent inspiration and ninety-nine percent perspiration."

❑   Zero Power sentences can begin with a humorous story:
*Fewer things are harder to put up with than the annoyance
of a good example. Mark Twain*

Purposeful beginnings

The reader and the purpose of your document will determine whether you use Zero Power sentences. Sales letters, marketing brochures, websites, executive summaries for investors or annual reports—all these need beginnings that capture your audience immediately.

You may use as many Zero Power sentences as you need to help introduce your topic and to cogently deliver your message to your reader. Do know that only ONE sentence in the beginning of your document can be the topic sentence. (Power 1) The rest of the sentences build interest, create excitement, or maybe just schmooze with the reader.

Here are some **examples** from print:

A direct mail letter:

*Does your firm lose income because your attorneys
do not bill all their time? Our clients have experienced
up to a 30 percent increase in billing revenue with our
Timekeeper software.*

From *Travel and Leisure* magazine:

Mention staying the night in a European castle and travelers are sure to have visions of the mansions of French kings and Spanish moors: canopied beds, well-trained valets, Aubusson tapestries. The castle hotels of Hungary are a species apart. Though slightly less luxurious than their western European counterparts, they nonetheless provide a rare opportunity to indulge in a rich man's vacation at a poor man's price.

Another mailer:

Steroids for Small Business! Pump up your business with high-speed DSL Internet service from... Free setup, free installation, free equipment.

Brochure cover:

Can HomeGrocer.com really simplify your life? Quite simply, yes.

Zero Power sentences:

✗ are usually included in your introductory (Power 1) paragraph

✗ add punch to your writing

✗ introduce your topic, product, or idea

I always write a good first line, but I have trouble in writing the others.

Molière

✗ provide necessary background information before launching into points

✘ alert the reader to important aspects of your report

✘ show warmth as well as relevance of information

✘ can stand alone or be integrated into your paragraph

✘ can greet or thank your reader

✘ may require that you revise your Power 1 sentence so that they flow together.

 ## *Practice: Now you try it*

Take any of the following topics and use any of the Zero Power approaches above to write Zero Power sentences for these topics. Here's one **example** to get you started.

1. A sales pitch for a new product

    Dear Dr. Julie Miller,

    More and more business owners are learning that the Internet is a very powerful tool. We at American Express Small Business Services are taking strides to harness the power of the Web and leverage it for our customers. The Small Business Exchange of- **Two Zero Power sentences and then the Power 1** *fers a wealth of information and professional advice that is sure to help you start, grow, and manage your business.*

2. A letter to your local representative favoring affirmative action legislation

3. An article urging voters to vote for the school bond or levy

4. An essay on the history of tae kwon do

5. A letter informing your patients that you are moving your practice

6. A proposal for the purchase of new telecommunications equipment

7. The opening comments to a business plan

Let's review the Zero Power sentences that have been added to the *time management habits* newsletter article in Chapter Two. The Zero Power sentences lead up to the Power 1 sentence* and combine with them to make an introductory paragraph—a Power 1 paragraph.

Zero Power (0) = *Imagine a bank that makes an $86,400 deposit daily into your account, but with a slight hitch—the balance does not carry over and the account returns to zero every night. Time is the same way: You have 86,400 seconds daily to spend any way you wish. They, too, do not carry over to the next day. How you manage those all-too-precious seconds and minutes will determine the quality of your life. *Practicing five indispensable habits can be your passbook to a full and rich life.*

The Power 1 sentence has been revised to flow with the entire paragraph. Read it aloud; you'll hear if it works.

Apply: You're on your own

Add Zero Power sentences to your document.

Let's continue with the beginning

Back in Chapter Two, we talked about specifying the number of points you'll be making in your document. However, you may decide that in the final draft you do not want to delineate the points in such a structured way. Putting a number in the Power 1 sentence is *not* a requirement. For **example**, the Power 1 sentence could be written:

Learning important time management habits can be your passbook to a full and rich life.

Your decision can also depend on:
- ❏ the document length
- ❏ the purpose of the document
- ❏ and your good judgement

PS: Unless you are creating a technical report, most documents you write will contain a Zero Power sentence. Even letters of rejection have one buffer statement (You were part of a large pool of outstanding candidates; however…)!

Here are **examples** of Power 1 sentences without a number.

❏ *Rhode Island and Pennsylvania illustrate the spectrum of economic development activity. (Insight)*

❏ *Necessary changes to the sales department will increase our revenue this next quarter.*

Look for additional ways to construct sentences in Chapter Four.

❏ *Our new customer service program keeps us competitive.*

❏ *While traveling in Europe, don't miss visiting these charming cities.*

THE BODY: MAKE IT ENGAGING!

The body of your document unpacks the information for the reader. Power 2 and perhaps Power 3 paragraphs comprise the middle section of your document along with transitions to guide the reader.

Depending on your purpose, the body may contain:

- ▶ technical data to prove your point
- ▶ methods described for carrying out a project
- ▶ details explaining why your approach is the best one
- ▶ budget details that show costs and justification for those costs
- ▶ personnel qualifications
- ▶ results expected
- ▶ evidence to persuade the reader
- ▶ facts that support the topic

Apply: You're on your own

Check out your body and see how it shapes up.

ENDINGS BRING YOUR DOCUMENT FULL CIRCLE

Seal your message with a Power 1

A Power 1 sentence or paragraph at the end of your document remains just as important as the one that begins your document. The poet William Yeats wrote about the sound of a finished poem. He described the noise to be like the click of a lid as it closed on a perfectly made box.

That same image applies to a concluding Power 1 sentence or paragraph. The document ought to end smoothly as well as click shut to drive home your points. Your ending can determine what remains in your reader's mind after he or she has finished reading.

> **I always wanted to write a book that ended with the word** *mayonnaise.*
> **Richard Brautigan**

A memorable quote, a powerful piece of evidence, a rhetorical question, a request for action, a summation of your points, a discussion of benefits are all techniques you can use in the concluding Power 1 sentence or paragraph.

Concluding Power 1 sentences/paragraphs—

❏ Can summarize your points to make sure your reader has stayed the course:

> *My suggestion is to read the proxy statement when it arrives to learn more about the company you own. When you are requesting information to study a company, ask for the proxy statement along with the annual report. It can be very revealing.*
>
> Better Investing

❏ Can restate or emphasize the main points without repeating the exact words that were already written:

> *Irving Kristol, reflecting on the lessons of the American Revolution, put it in a nutshell: "Self-government can only be achieved by a people who are capable of governing themselves."*
>
> The Seattle Times

❏ Can add a different twist or perspective:

> *These kids were brought up in a culture of violence, of denial of beauty, yet one kid says, "There's this spray of bullet holes over my door and it looks like a peacock's tail."*
> *...This astonishing image epitomizes poetry for me.*
>
> USC Trojan Family Magazine

❑ Can leave the reader thinking or questioning:

> *In the end, consumers and taxpayers will foot the bill for this fiasco.*
>
> The Seattle Times

❑ Can ask for action from the reader:

> *So what are you waiting for?*
>
> Food and Wine

 The type or length of your document will determine whether a concluding *Power 1* sentence or paragraph need be included. Use the chart below as a useful tool.

Power Guide

A concluding Power 1 sentence or paragraph is important in:

Application Letters	Last paragraph—a request for an interview, though not a formal/standard conclusion
Reports	State recommendations, etc.
Proposals	Formal proposals need recommendations; informal need only the last point stated
Letters	Be certain reader knows what future action will be taken

A concluding Power 1 sentence or
paragraph is NOT important in:

News/   Leave media contact information at start
Press Releases   of document regarding person/product/
                          business

Public Service   Present facts beneficial or helpful to pub-
Announcements   lic. For **example**, flu shot availability,
                          worthy fundraisers

Here is the concluding Power 1 paragraph in the *time management* newsletter article from Chapter 2. All the sentences combined make up the conclusion.

Concluding Power 1 Paragraph=*Anyone can acquire these five habits. Simple, tested, and proven in the real world of work, they can help you accomplish more in less time, thus freeing you for more enjoyable pursuits. Making time work for you remains the most important habit you can acquire in today's extraordinarily busy world.*

 Practice: Now you try it

Take any of these following topics and use any of the concluding Power 1 approaches above. Add a concluding Power 1 sentence or paragraph to these scenarios. Once again, I've given you an **example**.

1. The conclusion to your newsletter article

    The best move you can make is to talk to one of the professionals I've mentioned here. Working with a financial professional who is knowledgeable about the options available will benefit you in the short and the long run.

    The writer wrapped up the article succinctly in two sentences.

2. A letter responding to a customer complaint about services on board your airline

3. A letter responding to someone who has requested that his suspended driver's license be reinstated

4. A letter informing an interviewee that she did not get the position for which she applied

5. A letter of apology regarding an error in billing

6. A letter of application for a job

7. The final paragraph of your proposal

8. The conclusion to your newsletter article

 Apply: You're on your own

Add a concluding Power 1 sentence or paragraph to your draft. Also, reread your introduction. Does it now work with your conclusion?

 **Dr. Julie Tip:** If your document requires stating conclusions and that's difficult for you, here's a trick you might play on yourself. Instead of trying to summarize the conclusions, try just listing the most interesting or important findings. From that list you can then synthesize the information.

When you write with a group

If you're called on to create a document with the help of others, Idea Mapping and Power Numbers still work. Here's a few other tips for group writing:

 If you work best thinking through the topic alone before meeting with your group, give yourself a couple of days after all the research is in to absorb and analyze the information. Then you can formulate some conclusions before meeting with your group again.

 Try to limit the group to six people. More than that makes the process too complicated.

 Be sure key players and decision makers are in the loop. Waiting until the document is done is *not* the time to ask for feedback.

If you have grant writers, public information officers, or a marketing department, bring these experts in for a consult. They have an uncanny ability to quickly get to the point. Who knows, maybe they'll even offer to help write!

Feedback Is the "Breakfast of Champions"

Okay, now it's time to let someone else take a look at your document before your draft is finalized. *I cannot stress enough the significance of this step!* Letters, memos, reports, brochures, even important e-mails—any writing that will see the light of day—should be read by others before you send it off because—

❑ Feedback improves your final product even though it may drive you crazy, take time, or make you feel like you've bared your soul to the world.

❑ Feedback does not mean you have to give up your voice or throw out what you've written. Feedback does *not* equate with criticism.

❑ Feedback is getting another perspective—that of the different audiences who will read your document.

❑ Feedback means that when you hand the document over for review, you ask for specific suggestions from your reader, *not* just a pat on the back. By getting concrete answers to the questions below, you will be armed with crystal-clear ideas. Also, think about soliciting help from at least two people unlike you in personality.

Here are questions you might ask as you go about getting feedback from others:

- Have I been specific enough?
- Do I support my ideas with evidence that is objective?
- Do I present opposing points of view in an objective manner?
- Are you able to see the big idea?
- Does the document make sense?
- Is the document valid, accurate?
- Is the organization logical and sequential?
- How do you feel as you read this?
- Do I have examples that help the reader understand?
- Have I made a connection with you, the reader?
- Is my writing too detached and impersonal?

 Dr. Julie Tip: Make a feedback sheet with some or all of these questions. Clip it to your document and circulate. That way, you will get the feedback you want rather than ambiguous suggestions or vague praise.

Who you are professionally is mirrored in your writing. Taking time for feedback can avert the loss of revenue, image or clients. A superintendent of a large urban school district said, "I check my ego at the door and listen intently to the advice and ideas of others." A CFO of a large hospital concurred. "I will always ask others to read my material. The first question is 'What does this say to you?'"

QUICK AND EASY EDITING

What if you're not looking for comments on the *content* of your document? Maybe you just want someone to edit for those tricky grammatical and punctuation errors that we are all prone to make.

The story of an insurance company that failed to proof their documents will give you cause to sit up! As the woeful tale goes, the company wrote a rider for an existing policy and did not take time to go the extra mile. Unfortunately, *one* lonely sentence cost them hundreds of thousands of dollars, as it read: The company *is* liable rather than, *is not* liable.

So how to reduce time when you ask someone to review your document? Pass along a standard editing sheet. The "editor" saves time by not having to write out comments, and the writer *saves time* through reviewing the editor's shorthand rather than chicken-scratch comments in the margin. Some basic editing marks are below. Just be certain you all agree on them beforehand!

Mark	Meaning	Example
⟍	delete material	Be sure to proofread ~~the~~ your document.
(SP)	spell out	Refer to Chapter ③ for details.
⊃⊂	close gap	Zero Power sent ences are powerful.
⊃⊂ with slash	delete material & close gap	You can ac~~k~~quire a lif~~l~~ong skill.
stet.	return to original	Who says you can never ev~~er~~ break a rule?
∧	insert letter, word, phrase	You will learn to write *clearly, concisely, and* quickly.

change letter(s)	Avoid p̂assive voice.
add a space	Getting organized sav#es you time.
transpose letters/ words	Use an easel when working in a group.

Now review your entire document and consider the following questions:

A Writer's Checklist

✔ Does the Power 1 state the purpose of your document?

✔ Does your introduction capture your reader?

✔ Do your Power 2's (sentences or paragraphs) discuss your Power 1?

✔ Are enough examples and supporting points (Power 3's) included to help your reader understand?

✔ Does your conclusion restate the intent of the document without repeating the exact wording?

✔ By reading just your introduction and conclusion, would the reader know about your topic?

✔ Does the paper have logical organization?

✔ Do you maintain focus on your topic?

✔ Do the transitions help guide the reader?

In Summary

Rewriting is what good writing is all about. Take heart! Look at what these two writing experts said half-jokingly about the process of rewriting:

A clear sentence is no accident. Very few sentences come out right the first time, or even the third time. Remember this is a consolation in moments of despair.

William Zinsser

A lot depends on having the right spirit: businesslike and detached. A certain ruthlessness is best of all. Not desperate-ruthlessness, "Oh God, this is awful. I've got to change everything," but breezy-ruthlessness, "Yes, this certainly does have some problems."

Peter Elbow

WHAT'S NEXT?

In the next chapter, you will:

🖈 Review the C.L.E.V.R. solutions to business writing

🖈 Understand the importance of clear and concise writing

🖈 Learn what to avoid and what to eliminate

🖈 Practice adding a variety of sentence patterns

🖈 Use the six economical tips

🖈 Break some rules and follow others

Are we having fun yet?

CHAPTER FOUR

GET SMART

C.L.E.V.R. SOLUTIONS TO BUSINESS WRITING

I have good news and more good news! **One:** Merely reading your writing aloud can eliminate 60 percent of all your writing errors. That leaves only 40 percent you need to concern yourself with. **Two:** Out of that remaining 40 percent, you probably only have a few writing issues that you need to work on. **Three:** *Practice makes permanent.* If, as you review each of the C.L.E.V.R. solutions, you spend time practicing

Practice makes permanent!

them, they will then become a permanent part of your writing repertoire.

And no, C.L.E.V.R. is not a spelling error. It's a mnemonic device for helping you remember the solutions to your professional writing concerns. Mnemonics, a technique for improving memory, associates familiar words with new or unfamiliar words or concepts. Therefore, C.L.E.V.R. will help you remember the methods to use as you face your writing tasks. *A thought:* Use these solutions along with a good dose of common sense.

Remember: Everything in moderation. Your goal is productivity, not perfectionism. So, let's begin.

"C" STANDS FOR CLARITY

Clarity in writing results from good organization of your ideas. *Pat yourself on the back! Take a bow!* You've already accomplished *that* by using the Power Numbers system.

Clarity is also achieved by writing concisely and precisely. Choosing just the right word makes your intent clear to your reader.

> **Don't write merely to be understood. Write so you cannot possibly be misunderstood.**
> **Robert Louis Stevenson**

Consider the difference between these pairs of words:

profitable, productive
lucrative, well-paying
lost, forfeited
divested, ruined

> **A word is not a cystal: transparent and unchanged; it is the skin of a living thought and may vary greatly in color and content according to the circumstances and time in which it is used.**
> **Oliver Wendell Holmes**

Each has a slightly different definition. Being precise with your word choice aids your reader. So get out that dictionary and thesaurus!

Writing clearly and effectively means putting in specifics—time, place, numbers, or names—where appropriate. It just makes you that much more credible.

Which is more clear and precise?

Recently we have seen a gradual increase in profits.

or

Recently we have seen a 20 percent increase in profits.

Expressing exactly what you mean is the essence of clear writing and clear thinking.

Clarity means: Simplify your writing

In my seminars I tell participants that the pressure of time does not excuse unclear or confusing writing. It could cost a business time, money, energy, and prestige, and even a lawsuit!

Simple is best yet tough to do. These ponderously written **examples** desperately need repair!

 ## Practice: Now you try it

Turn these into simple, clear sentences:

1 A significant amount of the inventory appears to be improperly positioned in order to meet instantaneous shipping conditions. Furthermore, some portion of the quarterly lost sales was directly generated by the inability to effectively and efficiently transport our inventory.

2 We are enthusiastic about the opportunity to serve you and work with your people in this extremely important undertaking. We have the utmost confidence in our ability to help you to achieve a profitable organization through the repositioning of your market.

3 If you desire to have a modification as requested, you must apply to the appropriate department for this exemption. The requisite forms are attached and must be signed, dated, and returned. You should also plan to write this office as you were instructed in the letter of May XXXX.

Get your facts first, then you can distort them as much as you please!
Mark Twain

4 Due to the unexpected and continued high demand of our users covered under the Platinum Plan, it will now be necessary to change the rates by adjusting them effective July XXXX.

Some pretty clear stories

These tales from the front line help make my point.

☙ A telecommunication consultant stated that government RFP's are not granted without clear language. "Unless the reviewers can understand our specs, all our hard work gets tossed in the circular file!"

☙ A CEO of a large urban hospital says that clarity in communication is what he seeks in his writing. "I have to write responses to projects and programs undertaken in other areas of the country or other institutions. These documents require clarity of thought. The opposite has reflected negatively on me and my institution and destroyed our chances for funding."

☙ A hazardous-waste company got an unexpected surprise when the proposal they submitted to a longstanding client was rejected. They considered this a "no-brainer" contract, so they put out little effort and simply cut and pasted old verbiage. To their surprise, they lost out to the competition! Why? The words did not convey clearly and concisely that they could really do the job.

Try to see your words as you write so others may understand.

Clarity means:
Eliminate the ultimate weasel word: There

As you work to make your writing more clear, concise, and dynamic, eliminate the word *there* at the beginning of sentences. Its use does not produce engaging prose and should be expunged forever from your writing. A strong statement? No! *There*, virtually a non-word, can't really be diagrammed (wouldn't Sister be proud!) and can force you into using *to be* verbs.

Starting sentences *there is, there was, there has been, there will be*, and so on is simply a lazy way of writing. By removing this "weasel word," you will deliver your message more clearly and keep the reader interested.

Review the following **examples** and see how much brighter the sentences are without "there."

❑ There are five indispensable time management habits.
  Practicing five indispensable time management habits is your passbook to a full and rich life.

❑ There is a difference between the stated policy and actual practice in this organization.

A difference exists between the stated policy and actual practice in this organization.

❑ There are four money-saving ideas with our new customer service plan.

Our new customer service plan offers four money-saving ideas.

❑ There are several alternatives to this reorganization design.

Several alternatives to this reorganization design should be considered.

PS: You probably noticed that words were added to the sentences above. As you revise, be sure that your sentences still precisely state your intent.

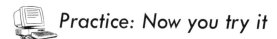 *Practice: Now you try it*

Rewrite these sentences, eliminating *there* at the beginning.

1. There are scads of scanners on the market, some really inexpensive. (*The Wall Street Journal*)

2. There are legal ramifications that go along with each 911 call.

3. There are three good stock buys in the technology sector.

4. There has been a lot of grant writing done in this department.

5. There is a clear definition for medical eligibility.

6. There's a lot that's cool about digital photography. (*The Wall Street Journal*)

7. There will be lots more before the dust settles. (*The Seattle Times*)

8. There's no telling what might be achieved in the next 1,000 years. (*The Seattle Times*)

Clarity means:
Saying no! to the verb "to be"

Beware of *to be* verbs such as *is, am, are, was, were, be, been, being.* Whenever you can, use more interesting, more specific, and more varied verbs than the ubiquitous old standby *to be.* I know, it's a tall order, but purge them from your sentences for these four reasons:

1 **They often introduce passive voice.**
Simply speaking, passive voice means that whoever performed the action gets second-class citizenship. For **example**, the sentence *The baseball was hit by Ken Griffey Junior* is passive. Ken did the hitting and he doesn't even get top billing! The baseball gets all the glory. To make the sentence active, you would write *Ken Griffey Junior hit the baseball.* (And probably over the fence!)

Think of passive voice as the opposite of active (as in action) voice. In active voice, the subject of the sentence performs the action, while in the passive voice, the subject is acted upon.

For **example** the sentence *The road was repaired by the construction crew* uses the passive voice. The people who actually did the work appear at the end of the sentence. Look what happens to the crew in the active voice: *The construction crew repaired the road.* In this sentence who performed the action is upfront.

2 **You get more bang for your buck and in fewer words!**
Eliminating *to be* verbs gives the reader more information with fewer words. By rewriting the sentences (in #1) above they became 20 percent shorter and much easier to understand! Count the difference in these two **examples:**

The letter was received by the manager. (passive)

versus

The manager received the letter. (active)

The second sentence in active voice is shorter, more direct.

The meeting was held by our department. (passive)

versus

Our department held a meeting. (active)

With active voice, you know upfront who performed the action.

 3 ***To be* verbs do your reader no favors!**
Eliminating as many of these verbs as possible will go a long way to making your writing more exciting and less wordy. When you write without using the *to be* verb as a convenient crutch, you force yourself to become more creative.

The active voice strikes like a boxer moving forward in attack; the passive voice parries while back-pedaling.
Theodore Bernstein

The following **example** illustrates this point.

The man was sitting on the bench. He was old and his skin was parched and wrinkly. I was about to speak to him when I noticed he was sleeping.

Now look at it rewritten with a minimum of *to be* verbs (and where used, they provide impact!)

The man sat on the bench, his parched and wrinkly skin a telltale sign of his advanced age. I approached him slowly, not wanting to startle him. Just as I started to speak, however, I noticed his closed eyes and heard his soft snore. He was dead asleep.

 To be verbs can cause confusion.
Look at this **example** from *Gregg's Manual of Style*:
A computer was reported stolen over the weekend by the security guard.

I smell **lawsuit**! The passive voice in this sentence unintentionally points a finger at the wrong doer!

By getting rid of as many *to be* verbs as possible you will accomplish two things:

❑ Your sentences will virtually leap off the page with fresh, vigorous language.

❑ Your sentences will become clear and concise.

Practice: Now you try it

Eliminate the *to be* (*is, am, are, was, were, be, been, being*) verbs in the following sentences.

1. The situation was studied by the committee.
2. Insurance is sold by this company.
3. Evaluation tools are used by our managers to keep our programs running smoothly.
4. Good writing is hard work.*
5. It was noted that it is believed that proposal "C" would be less expensive.

An important bird walk. Sometimes by simply changing the position of the words in the sentence, you can eliminate the *to be* verb. Other times, you will have to work a little harder. The first three sentences above are fairly easy to change, the fourth is a little more difficult. It could be rewritten: *Good writing involves/consists of/requires hard work.*

Is all passive voice wrong?

I hope I have made the case for active voice, which in most instances is the best choice. But is all passive voice usage wrong? Of course not! The key word in that sentence is *usage*. You don't want to go through verbal gyrations just to avoid all passive verbs, because the outcome may end up stilted or phony. The use of passive voice can work in the following situations:

1 In technical and scientific reports, it's the outcome that is most important rather than what effected the outcome. Therefore, the outcome is placed first in the sentence. By using passive voice you maintain objectivity. For **example**:

The volume of the fluid was decreased by 5 percent by adding sodium.

A new species of butterfly was discovered on the latest expedition to Central America.

The importance here is *what* was done not *who* did it.

2 Sensitive situations that require tact and diplomacy may dictate the use of passive voice. To avoid pointing fingers at the doer of the action in the following **examples,** which would you write?

Your sales team did not meet the quarterly profit goals.

or

The profit goals were not met this quarter.

The engineers created the defective plane parts.

or

The plane parts were made defectively.

In some instances the author may not be able to identify who did the action, or no doer is needed.

All the computer files were erased.

Mr. Brown was killed at a construction site.

Although you want to use active voice whenever possible, passive voice will creep into your writing. Just use it as you would expensive perfume—sparingly, provocatively, and in the right spots.

 Remember, common sense and moderation prevail. You do not have to completely eliminate *to be* verbs from your writing, just temper its use. Passive voice can be powerful. Could Shakespeare have written Hamlet's immortal lines—*To be or not to be: that is the question*—any other way and with such impact?

"L" STANDS FOR LANGUAGE

I've mentioned the importance of writing for your reader: keeping your tone, your voice, your words, the **language** in the document tailored to the specific audience. What to apply and what to abolish in your writing has been reviewed in previous chapters. Now I present **what to avoid**—and **what to use**.

Avoid clichés

Clichés fill business writing because of their obvious familiarity to the writer and the reader. However, relying on them can make your writing stale and uninspiring. *Water off a duck's back, the bottom line, few and far between,* and *which we would do well to bear in mind* are just a few **examples** of clichés. Avoid them as much as possible.

Last but not least, bite the bullet, take the ball and run with it while interfacing with the following **examples.**

Practice: Now you try it

Rewrite these tired clichés into fresher statements:
1. Of a confidential nature
2. Finalize
3. Venture a guess
4. At one fell swoop
5. Few and far between

Avoid jargon and acronyms

Jargon and **acronyms** are technical slang words (enterprise transformation initiatives) and abbreviations (NIMBY: Not In My Back Yard) unique to a particular occupation or group. They can be just fine and actually save time with in-house communication or when working with those in the same field. But remembering who your audience is will determine their use. Jargon and acronyms may be very clear in an e-mail sent to your peers, but you wouldn't think of using them with the board of directors.

If your document is going outside to those not in your field, confusion can set in. Consider these supposedly commonplace acronyms:

- CIA also stands for the Culinary Institute of America
- FBI is the acronym of a food and beverage organization
- NATO refers to a theatre owners' organization.
- COLA is governmentese for "cost of living adjustment"

Dr. Julie Tip: Technology writer Paul Andrews of *The Seattle Times* offers this suggestion: "If you're tired of decoding acronyms go to http:/www.mtnds.com/af/. Type in the acronym and the site searches through 70,000 acronyms and returns what it finds."

Avoid sexism

I don't need to go into any detail about this subject. Avoid sexist language. Period. Your purpose remains to inform, persuade, or sell, not offend. Here follows a list of some commonly used sexist terms with alternate suggestions:

Avoid	Use
anchorman	anchor
chairman	chair, chairperson, head
cleaning woman	domestic, housekeeper
draftsman	drafter
fireman	firefighter
foreman	supervisor
housewife	homemaker
mailman	mail carrier
mankind	humankind, humanity
newsman	reporter, journalist
policeman	police officer
salesman	salesperson
spokesman	spokesperson
stewardess	flight attendant
weatherman	weathercaster
workman	worker

 Always find out how people are to be addressed. Dr.? Ms.? Miss? Mrs.? Professor? Dean? Call and ask. If that's not possible, use Mr. or Ms.

Use descriptive writing

Yes, even in nonfiction writing, a turn of a phrase, a well-placed word can make the difference in the reader's receptivity to your message. Again, organization and clarity rule as you describe a process, a product, or a new service. But you also need to **choose and use** words that get the reader close to your writing.

Use Nouns

Using concrete **nouns** (Cadillac, book, piano) that appeal to one of the five senses is a good technique. I liken it to the Power Numbers system in that by using more tangible words you help the reader see, touch, feel, smell, or hear your idea. In contrast, abstract nouns do not provide the reader with a clear image. They name something intangible such as Judaism, poverty, love, courage. Look at these sentences below; which would help the reader get closer to the topic?

A product leaked on the floor.

versus

Gasoline leaked on the shop floor.

We store data.

versus

*We neatly store the mounds of information
piled in folders around your desk.*

Here are some descriptive noun **examples** from print:

A *New York Times* writer helped readers understand what the Mars rover, *Sojourner,* looked like by describing it as about *the size of a microwave oven.* And Walter Goodman from *The New York Times* wrote about Pat Buchanan: *His voice easily beats the enhanced decibel levels of the commercials.*

Use nouns that paint pictures for your readers. Avoid abstract ones that they can't wrap their brain around. Words such as *sad, gun running,* or *a billion dollars* conjure up more imagery than *emotion, crime, work,* or *wealth.* How will your descriptions help your reader?

Use similes, metaphors, analogies

Similes, metaphors, and analogies also work. These three figures of speech help the reader understand by comparing two unlike things. **Similes** are the most concrete of the three. With similes, the words *like* or *as* signal to the reader comparison while metaphors and analogies are subtler in their approach.

Similes

Two excellent simile **examples** come from James J. Kilpatrick's weekly column, "The Writer's Art":

From Chicago sportswriter Bob Verdi: *Trying to get a knee-high fastball past Smith is like trying to get a sunrise past a rooster.*

An *Arizona Republic* reporter wrote: *Suspects are as thick as ticks in timber.*

From the *San Diego Union Tribune*, a sportswriter described the city's annual Crew Classic: *As the shell crossed the finish line, the rowers collapsed like marionettes whose strings had been cut.*

Here a real estate tycoon is described in *Pacific Magazine*: *Bank accounts, stocks and bonds struck him as flimsy as sheets on a clothesline.*

Professor Stephen Hawking, the theoretical physicist, continues to garner recognition, according to Susan Page of USA Today. "Hawking's popular appeal seems to come from his…informal language and concrete metaphors. … He makes reasonably understandable such difficult and fundamental questions as the relationship of time and space."

Metaphors

Like similes, **metaphors** too can make your writing that much more inviting and energetic. Here is a metaphor **example** describing what a hotel did when its star chef announced he was leaving:

It turns its search machine on sizzle and sets out to find a replacement faster than a chocoholic can sniff out a double-decadence cheesecake. (*The Seattle Times*)

A metaphor **example** from *The New York Times*:

Hillary Rodman Clinton has fewer local roots than a giant cactus.

And from *The Washington Post*:

A reporter discussed a congresswoman "*with the voting record more middle of the road than a yellow line.*"

Just for fun

These mixed-up metaphors from Richard Lederer's book, *Anguished English*, humorously exemplify how metaphors can go awry:

- The slowdown is accelerating.
- When we get to that bridge, we'll jump.
- It's time to grab the bull by the tail and look it in the eye.
- I do hope that you don't think I've been making a mountain out of a mole hole, but that's the whole kettle of fish in a nutshell.
- Lou Brock, the great St. Louis Cardinal baseball player: *I always felt I was a guy who had the ability to light the spark of enthusiasm which unlocked the hidden geysers of adrenaline that causes one to play to the summit of his ability.*

Analogies

Analogies also serve as an excellent device when you are attempting to describe to the reader something unknown by describing something known. For **example**, again from James Kilpatrick's column, music critic Rita Landrum:

Although Watkins never seemed stiff, he did seem careful throughout the first half, as if he were driving a borrowed Lamborghini. He took it through its paces with great confidence and gave us a thrilling ride, but he didn't seem to own the car until after intermission.

Apply: *You're on your own*
Rework a document

Think about one of your products or services that you have previously described in some PR material, and see if you can rework it using strong, concrete nouns. Or practice writing a simile, metaphor, or analogy. Remember, take a familiar topic and add something dissimilar.

"E" STANDS FOR ECONOMY

Economy means don't waste the reader's time by telling them what they already know. Being brief but informative will always make you a winner. However, you do not want your writing to be so brief that it shows a lack

Whenever you can shorten a sentence, do. The best sentence? The shortest.

Gustave Flaubert

of thought; your reader still needs details. Rid your writing of rambling sentences, asides, any repetition of ideas for which you have already made your point. Shorten your words and your sentences. Economize. Make every word count. Pack the most meaning into the fewest words. Use these tips to get to the point!

"Don't dance with me!"

The owner of a large temporary placement service for the technology industry said that when he reads cover letters from applicants, the first words out of his mouth are often, "Don't dance with me. Get to the point! I'm busy, overwhelmed with the paper glut, and I don't have time to sift through your sentences to find out if your experience matches with my client's needs. Skip the frills, just give me the facts." (Thank you, Sargeant Friday!)

Dr. Julie Tip: Be careful that, as you make your points, you pick a few to focus on and go into depth. Unless you're writing a dissertation, depth is more important than breadth in writing.

Six Economical Tips

1 **Sentences should never be longer than 20 words.** Here's where reading your document aloud can help. If you're breathless by the end of a sentence, it's too long. Or count the number of words. Also, sentences can be one word. Honestly.

2 **One- and two-syllable words are best.** Again, the goal is to express ideas, not impress the reader with your vocabulary. Shorten words where appropriate.

Which of these are easier to see or hear?

Compare these words	To these
countenance	face
publication	book
utilize	use
perambulate	walk
domicile	home

 Avoid excessive use of *ion* or *ness*. Dropping these endings makes for stronger images in your sentences.

Rather than	Use
consideration	consider
conclusion	conclude
modification	modify
abbreviation	abbreviate
carefulness	careful
pompousness	pompous
indebtedness	indebted
greediness	greedy

 **Dr. Julie Tip:** Brevity is of the soul of wit and one way to keep your message brief is to resist the urge to create new jargon by adding the suffix *ize* to common words. For **example**, instead of *verbalize*, write say.

4 **Keep your paragraphs brief with only one idea per paragraph.** They give your reader's eye a break by providing white space on the page. When appropriate, paragraphs can also be only one sentence long.

5 **Use adverbs and adjectives frugally.** You need to lean on strong nouns and verbs as the framework for your sentences. However, often by adding adverbs or adjectives you create more accurate or complete images in the reader's mind. For **example**, *clear writing, confusing directions, haphazard growth, misspelled words.* These describing words clarify.

Be careful, though, because when overused or used improperly, adverbs and adjectives detract. For **example**, *most unique, definitely overcrowded, rather cloudy, less superb, supremely tragic.* These modifiers merely take away.

6 **Eliminate redundancy wherever you can.** Redundancy, the unnecessary repetition of words or concepts, appears so often in our writing that it may go unnoticed. Cut them from your writing. Some **frequently used redundant examples** follow. (Top of page 131)

Huh? So the question to be debated on both sides is: Should we refer back to the advance warnings, or postpone until later any further necessary requirements?

 In technical writing, the need for accuracy can make the reiteration of key points helpful to the reader. Though that may seem repetitive, you saw how effective (Chapter Three) the repetition of phrases can be. Just remember moderation. Don't cripple the impact of your words. Words have power and images; too many take away.

absolutely perfect	large (or small) in size
add up	my personal opinion
another additional	rectangular in shape
any and all	reduce down
cancel out	return back
combined together	the absolute truth
erase out	the month of May
fall down	yellow in color
hurry up	8 a.m. in the morning

 ## Practice: Now you try it

Rewrite the following phrases:
1. visible to the eye
2. 4:00 PM in the afternoon
3. the color of silver
4. cooperatively working together
5. immediately without delay

 ## Apply: You're on your own

What's write and what's wrong?

From what you have learned thus far, how would you write this letter? How would you respond if this were sent to you? Wouldn't you love the **opportunity** to strangle Dr. QRX?

Dear Ms. Hollinger:

I am writing this letter to notify my patients that I will be transferring from ABC Medical Center to XYZ Medical Center. I do this with mixed feelings because I have enjoyed the opportunity to participate in your health care, but the opportunity presented itself for me to cut back on my time commitments, affording me the opportunity to spend more time with my family.

I have the opportunity to share a practice with Dr. Doe and I look forward to this opportunity.

I would like to take this opportunity to thank you for the opportunity to participate in your health care.

Best wishes,

Dr. QRX

Dr. Julie Tip: Always print out your draft. It is easier to review from a hard copy than on the computer screen. Something about seeing the whole of it helps. Double-spacing the draft for ease of reading and revising is also a good idea. And make changes using a pen with colored ink so that your edits will be easy to pick up.

"V" Stands for Variety

I've recommended you read your writing aloud so you can hear what it really sounds like. Your ear remains the best guide for determining if you are maintaining a conversation with the reader. As you speak, your sentences have **variety** naturally. They ebb and flow, start with verbs, ask questions, etc. So, too, must your writing mirror that expressive variety.

Varying the construction of your sentences, as well as the length, is important; otherwise, you might put your reader to sleep! Variety means:

→ Don't anesthetize the reader!

→ Construct your sentences differently

→ Vary your writing style with sentence patterns

→ Creatively place punctuation as a way to add interest

Vary the structure

Did you know that sentences can be constructed in thirty-nine different ways or patterns? These different patterns make it easy to write interesting sentences. Therefore, you have no excuse for falling into the old subject-verb-object trap. Varying the pattern of your sentences is a technique that keeps your reader on alert.

Let's take a look at some **example**s of how a typical subject-verb sentence might be rewritten to give it more interest and power.

Here is the comfortable, standard style: *The third-quarter profits exceeded expectations.*

❑ You could ask a question:
    How much did the third-quarter profits exceed expectations?

❑ You could use a quotation:
    The chairman of the board gleefully announced, "The third-quarter profits exceeded my expectations!"

❑ You could begin with a preposition:
    During this third quarter, profits exceeded expectations.

❑ You could begin with an adverb:
    Giddily, the chairman described the third-quarter profits.

❑ You could begin with a gerund or -ing verb:
    Praising his sales force, the chairman stated that third-quarter profits exceeded all expectations.

❑ You could use an appositive:
    Mr. Ross, chairman of the board, announced the third-quarter profits.

In other words, vary your sentences. See how many different ways you can express the same idea!

The long and short of it

One strategy that professional writers use to create interest and variety is to place three or four long sentences together followed by a short sentence. This technique can make your writing seem more like a conversation. Or, you can reverse this process by placing a few short sentences before a long one as in this **example** from a phone company mailer:

Sounds great, doesn't it? Well, it gets even better. You can sign up for Call Forwarding from BellCo now and get one month FREE.

 You can't have every sentence sound the same. You would bore your reader to death. You would not sustain the interest of the recipient. Your monotonous words would put your reader's brain out to lunch. Your writing would lack interest and variety.

Are you still awake?

Parallel is powerful

Parallel structure also adds variety. Parallel structure is used when you are listing items within a paragraph or down a page. For **example**, discussion points for the next meeting, attributes of a new product, instructions to a client, or questions for an interviewee could be listed in phrases, or sentences, or with bullets, or with numbers. The key is that each phrase/sentence in the list must start the same way. If your list starts with verbs, all items on the list must start with verbs. If your list (below) starts with nouns, all items must start with nouns. **Examples** follow:

**What is written
without effort is, in
general, read without
pleasure.
Samuel Johnson**

We will work with you to determine what system best meets your needs, whether your goal is:

- *Improved customer relationships*
- *Reduced inventory costs*
- *Targeted one-on-one marketing*
- *Strategic business planning*
- *Customer notifications*

Parallel structure can also be used within a sentence. Again, the words or phrases must be the same. For **example:**

The bank offers savings, checking, lending, and trust services.

And coming back to Mr. Ross, the CEO (on page134), this is easy on the eyes and ears:

At the board meeting, Mr. Ross announced the profits for the third quarter, the names of the division supervisors, and the beginning date for the new product roll-out.

Dr. Julie Tip: This technique also works well when you are doing a résumé. List your accomplishments using parallel construction.

Combine your sentences

Another way to add variety to your writing is through **sentence combining.** Take two sentences that relate to each other and condense them into one. See how it works with these **examples:**

Read these sentences:

The old gentleman walked down the street. He was laughing. He saw a brown Labrador without a leash.

> **Often you must turn your stylus to erase, if you hope to write something worth reading.**
>
> **Horace**

Changed and combined it would read:

The laughing old gentleman walked down the street and saw an unleashed brown Labrador.

Let's look at a Power 2 paragraph from Chapter Two on *time management habits.*

Before:

Fourth, setting short- and long-range goals should be an ingrained habit. The process consists of deciding what levels of importance each of them have. Then you organize your tasks around achieving them.

After:

The last two sentences have been changed and combined: *The process consists of deciding the levels of importance of each and organizing the tasks around achieving them.*

Practice: Now you try it

Go back to your draft and look at your Power 2 and Power 3 sentences. Can they be combined? Look at your Zero Power sentence. Could it be revised to flow into your Power 1 sentence?

Punctuation adds punch!

Chapter Five discusses punctuation in detail. At this point, you just need to know that punctuation can speak for you. Since you are not speaking to your reader face to face, punctuation marks can take the place of gestures, voice inflection, and facial expressions. Dashes——, exclamation points **!** , question marks **?** , colons **:**, semi-colons **;** , and commas**,** all add variety and interest to your writing. They also provide signposts that guide your reader.

"R" STANDS FOR RULES

Some rules can be broken; others cannot. I've talked about breaking rules that get in the way of *getting organized* (Chapter One) and *getting started* (Chapter Two). Here are some you may want to follow:

A pessimist is a man who looks both ways before crossing a one-way street.

Lawrence Peter

1 Use a positive tone. How you come across to your reader, your attitude towards the subject—that is tone. Are you funny, terse, serious, formal, stiff, patronizing, rude, kind, positive? Knowing your reader is half the battle; the other half is avoiding words that may be negative.

Consider the opening sentence of this letter:

> Dear Ms. Bennett:
>   We regret to learn about your bad experience with our plant manager.

Now see what happens when you take out the negative words, state the facts as you see them, and change the tone to reflect a positive point of view.

> Dear Ms. Bennett:
>   Thank you for informing us that our plant manager was curt to you last week. He has asked that I send you his apologies. I have also enclosed the following information about your recent order.

Words such as *never, no, not, won't, can't, failed,* and other negatives need to be replaced with more positive words.

Some negative words to avoid:

failure	sorry	blame	misfortune
problem	complaint	impossible	misguided
intolerable	neglect	negligence	unfair
waste	weak	wrong	discredit
worry	careless	change	dispute
mistake	biased	exaggerate	unfortunate
abandon	cheap	evade	inefficient
low	senseless	vague	abrupt
useless	deny	ruin	pointless

2 | **Positively mind your manners!** Always remember *please* and *thank you.* Be courteous without gushing. More about etiquette in Chapter Five.

3 | **Be personable.** Keep *you* in your writing. Remember, if you depersonalize your writing too much, you won't make a connection with the reader. That's why using *you, he, she,* and *I* help build the rapport that words like *people, one,* and *individual* do not. Also, adding personal experiences creates interest. If that seems difficult for you, use quoted remarks from others.

Other ways to be personable:

➔ Let the reader know what you can do for him/her.

➔ If appropriate, use the reader's name in the body of the document.

➔ Hand write a "PS," if you can. People always read them!

Some rules to break

1 | Use fragments prudently.

We were taught that it was an unforgivable sin to write sentence fragments. Not always! Fragments are incomplete sentences and in certain circumstances work wonderfully. Fragments add interest or give emphasis. Just be certain the fragment relates to the previous sentence or thought. Here is an ad for Cartier:

Cartier. Now at Pacific Place.

Remember—use fragments sparingly and consciously.

2   **Use one-sentence paragraphs.**

It is a myth that all paragraphs must be three to five sentences long. One-sentence paragraphs can be very effective. They are often used in the beginning and ending of memos and may also be used between long paragraphs as a transition. One-sentence paragraphs exist in text with dialogue, and magazines often print one-word paragraphs! Check them out.

3   **Use inventive words (cautiously).**

Inventive words, called *neologisms* (meaning "new words"), can work. New words are being created almost daily. Some come from foreign languages (discotheque, pasta) or from technology (software, spamming) or from acronyms (scuba, laser) or are brand names (Xerox, Kleenex). Even nouns are coined as verbs: *Students **seminar** on books they're reading. Let's **calendar** our next meeting.*

In the recent edition of *Webster's College Dictionary*, many neologisms were recognized and defined. Here are a few more **example**s: *digerati* (someone knowledgeable about computers); *stork-parking* (parking for pregnant women); *aquadextrous* (to be able to turn the bathtub faucet on and off with one's toes); *netiquette* (code of courtesy on the Internet). Use neologisms like you would acronyms and jargon—judiciously.

4   **Begin with *but, and,* or *because.***

Beginning sentences with the above words can be quite effective when used for emphasis or transition. Here are some good **examples:**

- *And our new Money Market Account offers the best rates in town!*

- *I understand the difficulty that the imposed timeline has placed on your department. But we must still adhere to our deadline.*

- *Because of the high crime rate, Mayor Guiliani has taken extraordinary measures to clean up New York City.*

- *And he invites fellow citizens to call his new "Quality of Life Hotline" with a toll-free number.*

IN SUMMARY

In this chapter you worked hard! Remember you need not practice all the solutions. Some are already in your repertoire. Spend time only on those that feel a little shaky to you.

WHAT'S NEXT?

In the next chapter, you will:

🖈 Learn to avoid common business writing flaws

🖈 Recall punctuation basics

🖈 Review capitalization guidelines in business

🖈 Use the chronic misspelling guide

🖈 Examine e-biz writing

🖈 Use the Four Tips for sending professional faxes

And away we go!

Chapter Five

Get It Write

Prevent Disasters *Before* You Send Your Message!

Over the years, my clients have shared horror stories of the account, the client, the proposal, or the RFP that *got away!* In many cases, it boiled down to neglecting this important step in the writing process. Poorly placed commas, misspellings, errors in capitalization will cause lost revenue. "We worked three weeks on a huge bid for telephone equipment," said a telecommunications director. "With thirty minutes left, we did not proofread and misspelled the client's name. We lost the bid!"

Recovering lost revenue is easier than regaining one's reputation. Consider this story:

A young woman, an associate editor in a prestigious magazine, was seeking the next rung up on the career ladder. Discovering her "ideal" job on the Web, she began chatting via e-mail with the human resources director of this company. (*Chatting* is the operative word here.) Because of her informal style, and errors in spelling and punctuation, this woman was never taken seriously nor considered for the position. The human resource director explained it to her in no uncertain terms: "How could we *possibly* hire someone whose writing does not project the professionalism of our organization? Clean up your act, young lady!"

Who you are and what you stand for—your very credibility—is reflected in your documents. *Not* taking the time to make it right is like not combing your hair or dressing appropriately before you meet a client. *Of course* you'd take the time to look your best! Take the same care with your written communication.

You reviewed the **C.L.E.V.R.** solutions to business writing problems in Chapter Four. They focused on the *content* of your document. **Now** you need to pay attention to the *details* that can really make or break your professional image. Getting rid of any distracting flaws that may embarrass you, your company, or your boss is the theme of Chapter Five. So . . .

You need to proofread like crazy!

Proofreading can avoid such mistakes as these:

I collided with a stationary truck coming the other way.

I had been driving for 40 years when I fell asleep at the wheel and had the accident.

The pedestrian had no idea which direction to turn, so I ran over him.

About two years ago, a wart appeared on my left hand, which I wanted removed.

Anguished English

Dr. Julie Tip: On very important documents, you might consider reading your writing backwards. Tedious though it may be, this proofreading technique works. By reading backwards, you cause your brain to stop and question "the sense" of your words. Therefore, you have a better chance of catching mistakes.

This chapter is divided into four sections:
- Punctuation basics
- Capitalization highlights
- Spelling suggestions
- E-biz writing

Each of these make the point—get it *write* before you send your message!

THE BASICS OF PUNCTUATION

You know how to use periods, exclamation points, and question marks, which are all fairly straightforward, so let's look at punctuation perplexities that could make or break you.

A birdwalk: Most punctuation usage is based on two things: personal choice and reader understanding. You need to know **the basics**. However, I recommend the following books for **the specifics**: *The Well-Tempered Sentence* (Karen Gordon); *Write Right!* (Jan Venolia).

The Comma

The **comma** is the most widely used and abused of all punctuation marks. Here are some general guidelines:

 Use a comma after a long introductory phrase or clause.

Contrary to common belief, English women do not wear tweed nightgowns. Hermione Gingold

I've been on so many blind dates, I should get a free dog. Wendy Lieberman

If the introductory phrase is short, no comma is needed:
After the dinner I went home.

2 **Use a comma to avoid reader confusion.** Try reading this sentence out loud without the comma. You'll *hear* the problem.

Once you understand, the reason is clear.

If he chooses, Williams can take over the company.

3 **Use the comma to separate items that are listed.**

Early to rise and early to bed makes a man healthy, wealthy, and dead. Ogden Nash

The only way to keep your health is to eat what you don't want, drink what you don't like, and do what you'd rather not do. Mark Twain

: Both of these **examples** have a comma before *and*. It is up to you whether you use one here. However, in these **examples,** the comma forces the reader to pause and consider the punch line.

Other times, the comma can prevent confusion as in this **example**: *The farmer has three kinds of cows for sale. They are black, brown and black and brown.*

The buyers are probably scratching their heads—how many cows and how many colors? Placing a comma after *brown* would quickly clear up this mystery.

 Use a comma to separate complete sentences that are joined with a conjunction: *and, but, for, or, nor, yet,* or *so.*

The optimist proclaims that we live in the best of all possible times, and the pessimist fears this is true. James Branch Cabell

Everybody talks about the weather, but nobody does anything about it. Mark Twain

5 Use a comma(s) to separate nonessential phrases from the rest of the sentence. The words between the commas may be deleted, and the sentence still makes sense.

Unlike Andy Rooney, who puts out a book every year, I at least have the courtesy to wait two years before I offer something new. Art Buchwald.

Pessimism, when you get used to it, is just as agreeable as optimism. Arnold Bennett

Use a comma when you are directly addressing someone.

Reader, suppose you were an idiot. And suppose you are a member of Congress. But I repeat myself. Mark Twain.

Dr. Livingstone, I presume? Sir Henry Morton Stanley

7 Use a comma between a proper name and a title or explanatory phrase (appositives). Appositives are words that follow nouns or phrases and give further information. They, like parenthetical phrases, are not necessary for the sentence to make sense, but are informative to the reader.

Bill Gates, Chairman of Microsoft, spoke in Las Vegas last month.

My son, the orthodontist, sent me flowers for my birthday.

Let us be grateful to Adam, our benefactor. He cut us out of the "blessing" of idleness and won for us the "curse" of labor. Mark Twain

8 Use commas to separate items in a geographical address.

Positano, Italy

10 Glandore, Dalkey, County Dublin, Eire

 Use commas with quoted material.

John Kenneth Galbraith said, "Nothing is so admirable in politics as a short memory."

10   *Do not* use commas to separate the subject of the sentence from the verb.

Upfront discussions, save a lot of grief.

This can also cause misunderstanding when a long phrase occurs before the verb.

Traveling, reading, and gardening, are my three favorite pastimes.

 Remember, the technique of putting a comma where you naturally pause is okay *most of the time.* The above basics will help you with the rest of the time.

Grammarians are renowned and reverberated.

Get Thee to a Punnery

The colon

The **colon** is used to alert the reader. It signals: *Okay here comes information.* It introduces a list or a quote or an explanation. It takes the place of the words *that is* or *for example.* The colon is also sometimes used to open a business letter when you do not know the recipient.

In two words: im possible. Samuel Goldwyn

Zsa Zsa Gabor once observed: "I am a very good housekeeper. Each time I get divorced I keep the house."

On a divorce lawyer's wall: Satisfaction guaranteed or your honey back.

Dear Sir or Madam:

Use a colon after *as follows* or *following.*

The ingredients of a diplomat's life have been identified as follows: protocol, alcohol, and Geritol.

The semicolon

The **semicolon** is the odd duck in the world of punctuation. It's neither a period nor a comma, but a little bit of both. More formal than the colon or the dash, it forces the reader to pause. A semicolon separates two main clauses, each forming a complete thought. Since the clauses are closely related they are better joined together with a semicolon. Using *and* or a period would not have the same impact.

When angry, count four; when very angry, swear. Mark Twain

In politics, if you want anything said, ask a man; if you want anything done, ask a woman. Margaret Thatcher

Freedom is never voluntarily given by the oppressor; it must be demanded by the oppressed. Martin Luther King, Jr.

Semicolons can also be used to:

❑ Separate a list of complex items:
Persons attempting to find a motive in this narrative will be prosecuted; persons attempting to find a moral in it will be banished; persons attempting to find a plot will be shot. Mark Twain

❑   To separate clauses that have commas:

> At my 50th birthday party, the caterer prepared a vegetable basket with two dips, ranch and dried tomato; assorted imported cheeses, including Gruyère and brie; a fresh shellfish bar with clams, oysters, and scallops; a pasta bar with six sauces; and three different desserts.

Old grammarians never die—they just lose their verb and slip into a comma.

Get Thee to a Punnery

The dash

The **dash** can be a dramatic tool *if* used sparingly. Be careful here as it says to the reader abruptly, *I'm now going to make a strong statement—one that I want you to pay attention to.* It places additional emphasis on an idea and can be used like a comma, colon, or parentheses. You are hereby officially warned about its misuse.

> *It's not the men in your life that count—it's the life in your man.*
> Mae West

> *A classic—something that everybody wants to have read and nobody wants to read.* Mark Twain

> *I think—therefore I'm single.* Lizz Winstead

PS: Some word-processing programs turn two hyphens into a long dash (—) if you type them together. Otherwise, always use two hyphens. You decide; just be consistent.

The Parentheses

These are even *less* formal marks than the dash. They mean to be an aside, something that you would whisper to the reader. They make the reader pause so that you can tell them something chatty, interesting or helpful *but* not essential to your document. If you don't care whether the reader pays attention to the information in the **parentheses**—fine. If you do care—don't use them. Your sentence should make sense even if the information in the parentheses was deleted.

For God's sake (I never was more serious) don't make me ridiculous any more by terming me gentle-hearted in print. Charles Lamb

My old grannum (rest her soul) was wont to say, there were but two families in the world, have-much and have-little. Miguel De Cervantes

PS: Unless what is written inside the parentheses is a complete sentence, put any punctuation marks *after* the parentheses. Check the recommended books above for variations.

Quotation marks

Quotation marks are mostly used just as their name suggests: to show the reader what was said "exactly." They can add interest, variety, or credibility to your document.

When someone exultantly exclaimed, "Eureka!" Chico Marx shot back, "You donna smella so good yourself!"

"No, Eve, I won't touch that apple," said Tom adamantly.

Other uses of quotation marks are:

❑ To enclose a word or phrase that is being defined:

The two most beautiful words in the English language are "Check enclosed." Dorothy Parker

❑ For words with special meaning:

"Idea Maps" can help you quickly organize your conference speech.

❑ To identify titles of articles, essays, poems, short stories, songs, or chapters.

"Five Indispensable Time Management Habits"

Italics

Thanks to the shift from typewriter to computer, the use of **italics** has gained popularity. Where once you underlined, now italics are used. Italics show emphasis, signify titles, or identify foreign words that are not readily recognized by the reader.

❑ Italicize titles of books, periodicals, newspapers, movies, paintings, television shows, plays, magazines, long poems, ships, trains, and aircraft.

The Wall Street Journal   *The Honeymooners*

Crossing to Safety   *The Concorde*

❑   Italicize unfamiliar foreign words.

Our exchange student from Italy used the word *andiamo* which means "let's go!"

Apostrophe

The much-maligned **apostrophe** gets as much abuse as the comma. The confusion seems to be mostly around possessive nouns and contractions.

❑   Use an apostrophe to signify ownership/possession:

The manager's paycheck = the paycheck belongs to the manager

One frog to another: Time's fun when you're having flies.

Writer's block = the block belongs to the writer

Get Thee to a Punnery

❑   Use an apostrophe only for plural possessives when the noun ends with an s:

Garbage drivers' strike

Engineers' new salaries

❑   Use apostrophes to signify contractions, where two words are combined to make one and a letter or letters are dropped. For **example:** it's = it is. The apostrophe takes the place of the letter *i*. If you find it easy to make this mistake, just read the word as if it's (it is) two words. *Its* is a possessive. It's important to know the distinction between these two.

Some everyday contractions:

I'm=I am	doesn't=does not
I'll=I will	they've=they have
isn't=is not	s/he's=s/he is
aren't= are not	you've= you have
can't= cannot	

I've been called many things, but never an intellectual.
Tallulah Bankhead

 Remember possessive pronouns do not use a contraction:

Hers, his, its, theirs, ours, yours, whose.

Life is for each man a solitary cell whose walls are mirrors.
Eugene O'Neill

❑ Use apostrophes to show omission of one or more letters in a word or a number:

Th' only way t' entertain some folks is t' listen t' 'em. Kim Hubbard

Class reunion of '65 (1965)

PS: Since deciding where to put apostrophes makes most of us crazy, one of the referenced source books will come in handy.

Hyphens

The **hyphen** is most often used to join compound words that have a relationship with each other: brother-in-law; self-love; editor-in-chief. Hyphens can also clear up misunderstandings.

For **example**, hyphens would have helped in these headlines:

Eye drops off shelf

British Left waffles on Falklands

Squad helps dog bite victim.

Hyphens are used for compound numbers from twenty-one to ninety-nine. Hyphens also occur after these prefixes: self, ex, all.

If prefixes used for a common element are listed in a sentence, insert a suspending hyphen.

The teenage girls pranced in front of the mirrors in their maxi-, midi-, and miniskirts.

Take out an 8 1/2- by 11-inch piece of paper.

Formatting

Formatting your document is a proofreading necessity. Your document needs to be as easy on your readers' eyes as your words are on their ears. Being able to quickly scan a document tops most readers' lists.

Conversely, if readers have to plow through your dense text, your document will surely be put at the bottom of the pile. You're just making it too tough and time-consuming to get through your words! So visually lay out your text so that it appeals, looks attractive, and is appropriate. **I promise** you will win immediate friends.

Review this practical checklist each time:

✔ Is the document layout attractive and appropriate?

✔ Is white space used so that key ideas stand out?

✔ Are graphics used where needed to help instruct the reader?

✔ Are the visuals straightforward and simple?

✔ Does all accompanying text to the visual clarify and/or explain?

✔ Are typographic devices (such as bolded words, italics, underlining, bullets, font size) used for key points in order to guide the reader?

Capitalization

As with punctuation, you already know the basics to capitalization. Just as a reminder, I have listed persons, places and things that need to be capitalized. Check those reference books for additional specifics.

Capitalize the following:

❑ Names and initials for persons

Anthony E. Smith   Dr. Mary Lynne Derrington

❑ Places, geographical areas

San Marino, California   the South   Europe

❑ Organizations and their members, corporations, government agencies

Dept. of Corrections   Rotarians   Junior League

❑ Ships, planes, and spacecraft

The Crystal Harmony   Voyager II

❑ Ethnic groups, races, religions, languages

Jewish   Italian   Muslim   Farsi

❑ Days, months, holidays, historical periods/events

Monday   August   Fourth of July   Boston Tea Party

❑ First word in a quote

Humorous writer, Dorothy Parker, said in a theatre review, "She runs the gamut of emotions from A to B."

❑ Book titles, articles, plays, films, reports, poems, works of art, musical compositions

Business Writing That Counts!   Les Miserables

Saving Private Ryan   The Pietà   La Bohème

❑ Trade names

Band-Aid   Coca Cola   Q-Tip   Windows 2000

Spelling

Spelling can intimidate even the best of us, as rules, and exceptions to those rules, abound. Fortunately, most word processing software has spell-check. *That,* as you know, *does not* excuse you

from proofing your document before it goes out! Misspelled words can project a poor image or inaccurate information. Peruse these dillies:

The choir will meet at the Larsen home for fun and sinning.

Save regularly at our bank. You'll never reget it.

Misspelled words can also cause confusion as in these sets of words: *stationery* or *stationary*; *principle* or *principal*; *affect* or *effect*.

Two suggestions to help you with your spelling:

1 **Keep that dictionary close to your computer.** If you don't know how to spell the word that you want to look up, think of a synonym for that word.

2 **Keep a list of words that you frequently misspell.** You might even try to memorize them. For **example**, the word stationery (materials for writing or typing) is really tough for me to remember. So I memorized it by relating it to the word paper. The *er* at the end is my clue to its spelling.

Here is a list of some commonly misspelled words:

accept/except	appointment	calendar
accommodate	appreciate	catalog
achieve	assignment	certain
acknowledge	assistant	challenge
adjustment	authority	circumstance
advertisement	balance	clientele
advice	bargain	color
agreement	beneficial	commercial
allotted	brochure	commission
all right	budget	committed
answer	business	competition

conference	hoping	possible
confidential	identical	practically
congratulate	illegible	preferred
consequence	immediately	procedure
consensus	inconvenience	professor
continuous	individual	realize
convenience	inquiry	really
courteous	instead	receipt
courtesy	interrupt	receive
customer	knowledge	recommend
decision	language	reimburse
definitely	liability	respectfully
dependent	library	ridiculous
development	license	salary
dilemma	listen	satisfactory
dissatisfied	maintenance	Saturday
doubt	making	secretary
economical	mayor	separate
efficiency	meant	sincerely
eliminate	mileage	sufficient
embarrass	miscellaneous	technique
emphasize	misspell	temporary
enough	monotonous	their
enthusiastic	mortgage	thorough
especially	necessary	though
excellent	negotiate	tomorrow
experience	noticeable	truly
facilities	oblige	unfortunately
February	occasion	unique
finally	occurrence	unnecessary
foreign	opportunity	usable
fortunate	original	useful
generally	pamphlet	usually
government	participant	vague
grammar	particularly	various
guarantee	patience	Wednesday
guess	permanent	writing
hazardous	personnel	written
height	persuade	yesterday

E-Biz Writing

E-Everything!

Everywhere you look, we've gone "E" crazy! E-business, e-music, e-zines, e-services, e-banking, e-shopping, e-filing, e-stamps, and—the *beat* goes on! Who could have predicted this breathtaking, sky-rocketing growth?! Just two years ago when the first edition of this book came out, I stated that 40-plus million people had e-mail. A paltry sum compared to today's over 183 million users! *And,* even as I share the future forecast for Internet use, these numbers will be out of date. But alas, I must carry on. Take a look:

According to the Massachusetts Institute of Technology Enterprise Forum, over the next five years, the number of people using the Internet is projected to grow by:

> 297% in Asia
>
> 234% in Western Europe
>
> 404% in South/Central American
>
> 155% in North America

A cyber story: An information services manager told of a user who couldn't open her attached e-mail files. She was instructed to "right mouse click," but still couldn't do it. Frustrated, the manager came to inspect the computer and saw the words "mouse click" written repeatedly across the screen. "You told me to write 'mouse click,'" the user explained.
The Wall Street Journal

These numbers *do not even* touch the astounding growth expected in e-commerce. By the year 2003, according to International Data Corporation, Internet sales will reach into the trillions with 50 percent of the sales occurring *outside* our borders. (And e-commerce is only three or four years old!)

Along with these numbers comes the stunning speed of technology progress. PDA's (Personal Digital Assistant) are selling like proverbial hot cakes and high availability is the new norm. A recent radio commercial pushed the latest product, "You can stay connected 24/7 and at 240 times faster than ever before. No down time necessary!" The very thought of being perpetually plugged-in with the world puts some of us right over the edge.

So, this gift from the geeks and the bane of our existence is changing everything. How we do business, how we communicate, how we work, how we establish relationships, how we make purchases. Its omnipresence grows hourly.

According to Brain Reserve, 40 percent of all employers presently offer telecommuting. And by the year 2005, at-home workers will number 21 million.

An oxymoron

Everyone is touting the electronic revolution—the speed, the instancy of the Internet has caught us up in its quickness and velocity. Every possible superlative is being thrown at it. Cyber-communicating is hyped as the e-pitome in connectedness. It is considered the *best thing since sliced bread; the only way to fly.*

However, I challenge the description of this new icon as *the missing link to good communication*. I would like to suggest that the label *e-mail communication* might be an oxymoron. The very nature of e-mail is to be fast. But fast does not necessarily equate with *better*. Shortcuts on the information highway can be risky, as they may not supply good, crisp communication. Fast *can* also equate with sloppiness, errors, and cutting corners you would *never* normally cut.

So, if you believe that clear communication is important for understanding, for business growth, and for building relationships, I invite you to *slow it down* and *make it right* before you press *send*.

Everybody's writing

I have even more good news, and—some bad news. The good news: *everybody's writing*. The bad news: *everybody's writing*.

Yes, e-mail has encouraged people to write again. The written word is alive and well over the Internet. We are recording what we do and think as well as keeping in contact with friends and family.

Even teenagers are spending more time "chatting" online than talking on the phone.

But the bad news is that you have no place to hide if writing is not your strength. Everyone is expected to write and respond to the customer. In the good ole days we had a secretary (or at the very least a secretarial pool down the hall). No more! If you have access to a computer, you're supposed to log on and let the words fly. Therein lies the danger, as miscommunication can cost you time, money, even your reputation.

A sad cyber tale

A well-known financial institution was experiencing morale problems—complaints were up, productivity was down. Through a communications audit, the main culprit was revealed: their online internal newsletter. So boring and poorly written, no one read it. Miscommunication was rampant and employees were finding out the good, bad, and ugly on the streets from their competitors. In response, the phones in the head shed started ringing: *What's this I hear about a rate increase? Why is Sam leaving marketing? Why are we reorganizing, again?*

The consequence? A tremendous amount of incalculable waste: waste of *time* to explain what really was the truth; waste of *money*—just calculate the cost of productivity lost as each call was responded to; waste of *reputation*—to justify why *you* hired this team to write the newsletter in the first place. And what about those missives that went out to your customers, the ones you didn't see or know about?

So Beware! E-mail may be hazardous to your career, your business, and your future, because good writing is good writing no matter what the medium. Proofing what you write before you press *send* should become second nature.

The guidelines offered in this chapter and book extend to all electronic communication. Although I am certainly not an e-mail expert, the following are offered in the spirit of good communication. Below e-mail tips and suggestions are organized around four topics:

- Composing your message
- Contemplating your audience
- Controlling your time
- Considering what medium

COMPOSING YOUR MESSAGE

Commit this to memory—a human being sits at the other end of your message. Don't forget that fact in your need for speed.

❑ **Stand out above the noise.** Compose a short and catchy phrase for the subject line. Focus it on the content of your message. Think newspaper headlines. They capture in a few words the essence of the article.

❑ **Use those Power Numbers!** List the Power 2's upfront; your reader can then scroll down for the details.

Roni,

   Two key decisions need to be finalized at our next meeting:

   *IPO drop-dead date for filing

   *Public relations blitz

   If you need to review some background information see below.

Heather

   **********For Your Information (FYI) **********
   Detailed information can be placed below this line.

❏ **Bulleting your key points and the required action** at the top of your message can help your recipient quickly scan. Since everyone has a different system, use either the asterisk * or these *doo-hickeys* << >> to draw attention.

❏ **Avoid long-winded messages.** Be clear, concise, and to the point. Use the long-standing journalist rule of the five W's (who, what, when, where, and why) when constructing your message.

As a little girl climbed onto Santa's lap, Santa asked the usual, "What would you like for Christmas?" The child stared at him open-mouthed and horrified, then gasped, "Didn't you get my e-mail?"

❏ **Short and sweet** means only one screen-size amount of text, which calculates to no more than 800-900 words. And choose a font that's easy on the eyes. Since it takes 25 percent longer to read text on screen than it does on paper, do your reader a favor.

❏ **Think through your message.** Important ones that need some reflective time are better left to be sent later. This gives you time to proof, calm down, or be sure your message will not be misinterpreted.

❏ **Don't forget to let your reader know what you want them to do** with your message. Using the acronym *RSVP* is a shortcut that can guide your recipient. OR, type in the words *Action Item* and enumerate the activities before the body of text.

❏ **Compose a professional signature and e-mail address.** You are what you write. Your sig. file (signature file) should contain contact information only, not cutesy sayings or whimsical words of wisdom. The same caution applies to your e-mail address—be professional and appropriate.

CONTEMPLATING YOUR AUDIENCE

☐ **The important (but impatient) reader:** The responsibility for the message lies with YOU, the sender. Since readers tend to scan e-mail text, always ask yourself: Who really needs this information? You want to add value to your customers, not junk up their in-box. So write with a *purpose in mind*, not *just because*.

☐ **Remember to whom you are sending your message.** The formality of your writing style (or lack of) will be determined by who the recipient is. That does not give you permission to ignore all writing conventions. As you know, e-mail does not go unseen, even in the privacy of your own home. I don't know about you, but I always print out important e-mails and they sometimes sit around the office, available to lots of eyeballs.

To some people, informality means no punctuation, spelling, capitalization, or grammar. A conversational tone is fine; this virtual lack of regard for the King's English is not:

> **The paper industry predicts a six-fold increase in white paper production in the next five years.**

The presentation was this morning Iputtogether some scatted thoughts on paper late yesaterday afternoon and I hope that one of them will fly they are very borad concepts...If see then we need a serous 5 page proposal. ..FJUst got the form the foundatino.

❑ **Always greet your reader.** Address your recipient with greetings such as *Hi, Linda,* or *Team* for informal messages.

❑ Formal salutations are needed for more professional correspondence. Most important, **please and thank you** have not gone out of style. Remember these niceties in your message.

❑ **Don't catch a virus!** Attachments are risky business. People open them without knowing who is sending them. Even with family and friends, never open an attachment unless you have scanned for a virus.

❑ **If you reply to a message that has an attachment,** be aware that the attachment will not be included in your reply. If you have modified the attachment, forward the reply or compose a new message.

❑ **Emoticons:** These are graphic representations of emotions; for **example,** :) signals *happy,* : (signals *sad,* :o means *bored. Some* hit most people the wrong way; others cannot be understood, such as **$-)** = *just won the lottery;* or I-(= *late night message;* others could offend, like : - (*) = *about to vomit.* Drive carefully!

❑ **Junk mail can overwhelm the recipient.** How much attention do you pay when it comes through snail mail? If you are a *spammer,* watch out as organizations are cracking down on this useless verbiage flying through the air. When sending any correspondence, be sure the recipient is interested in its content.

❏ **Sending jokes can brighten someone's day**, but be sure the recipient sees this practice as being as valuable as you do. Jokes are junk mail to some. For them, nothing is more annoying than being on someone's joke mailing list. If you are a joke sender, pre-qualify your message by asking them: "Do you want to be on my list?" This gives them the opportunity to say no.

PS: Be sure your jokes are clean enough for everyone to read because it's a good bet they will be passed on— along with your name attached. Companies are increasingly concerned about harassment charges if the wrong person is exposed to the message.

❏ **Forwarding raw data** to others is not a good idea. It can take too long to download, some systems can't handle that much data, and most people are not interested.

❏ **Threading—pros and cons:** Since we are all on information excess, don't assume everyone remembers your previous conversation. Sometimes threading your discussion helps. On the other hand, it creates lengthy text that has to be waded through to get the point. Instead, copy and paste the pertinent information into your reply.

CONTROLLING YOUR TIME

I bet you are now receiving more e-mail messages than you are phone calls. Abide by the same rules for managing your e-mail that you would snail mail that crosses your desk: *Handle it only once!*

And hold on for these projections: Analysts at Forrester Research predict that by the year 2005, the daily count of e-mail messages will hit 5 billion. According to John R. Quain, contributing editor at *Fast Company*, "Those numbers only measure personal e-mail traffic; including business e-mail could increase the total exponentially." Closer to home, a recent client of mine in charge of his company's website said that in a three-day period, he received 3,600 e-mails!

So seriously consider these suggestions:

❑ **Manage your e-mail.** Use programs like Microsoft's *Outlook Express* or Qualcomm's *Eudora* to manage your e-mail. Prioritize the folders according to the project you're working on or the message frequency from one client. For **example**, I do a fair amount of individual coaching in writing, so I have a folder for each client with his/her writing samples.

❑ **Make a deal with yourself** that you will check your e-mail at least twice day. You would certainly do this with your voice mail and the same consideration should apply to e-mail. This will allow you to handle your messages in a timely and professional manner without being chained to your computer. E-mail messages, like phone messages, should be returned within twenty-four hours.

PS: Don't multi-task while you're reading your e-mail. You end up having to reread it because of your lack of concentration, and thereby wasting your valuable time.

❑ **Don't make assumptions about other people's time.** Everyone has a different system of checking e-mail. Some people are connected all day and others may check only once or twice a day. If it's really important, call the person and leave a message. Let them know they can refer to your e-mail message for details.

❏ **Be considerate.** You may be overwhelming others with the number of communications that you send. Try sending just one acknowledgement from the multiple messages of your sender.

A Wayne McKinnon tip from his book, the *Complete Guide to E-Mail*: For a brief response, just writing in the subject line may be enough to provide the reader with information:

From: Vicki
SUBJECT: Good luck and happy editing!

CONSIDERING WHAT MEDIUM

The facts speak for themselves. We have moved to a global economy which means we are communicating with people all over the world. Though the ease and convenience of e-mail can be appealing, cultural mores may dictate otherwise. In some countries, it is considered very bad form to have an electronic communiqué be the first contact with the client.

Therefore, think about what medium works best with what customer. Here are some considerations as you choose your communication vehicle.

1 **Level of rapport:** Do you know your customer well enough that e-mail is the correct mode? Because people are not receiving verbal and nonverbal cues, messages can be misconstrued.

When we speak with someone, we obviously see their gestures, hear their tone of voice, and can read them a lot better than via the Internet. Even a phone call can be the better option.

2 **Importance of message.** Do you have bad news? Delivering it via the Internet is a no-no.

3 **Confidential nature of message.** Be careful as all e-mails can be retrieved. If it's private and you don't want the message published in the paper or read by your mother, don't write it!

4 **Skill level of the user.** Your recipient may not be as fluid as you with their e-mail skills. Take that into consideration before you choose your medium for your message.

That personal touch is still important whether you're addressing a client or a co-worker. John Naisbitt's prediction ten years ago in his best-selling book, *Megatrends*, that *the more high tech, the more high touch* is necessary, is still a basic premise to any communication.

A training manager commented on this problem. "The biggest problem I have with e-mail is when one of my supervisors uses it. He's well-intentioned, but he is not the best writer and forgets that e-mail does not have the inflection and nuance of the spoken word. As a result, I've had to go down to the director's office and reassure her that he was not being sarcastic or insubordinate—that's just the way he communicates!"

FAXES

For very important messages, try sending a fax. The beauty of a fax is that no problems occur regarding losing attachments. But do remember, just as e-mail is not *for your eyes only*, the same goes for faxes. In fact they can be very public. Sender take note! Faxes usually arrive hand-delivered to the person's desk. Therefore, many may see confidential or sensitive material before it reaches your desk. Employ all the above tips when you fax any document.

Additional suggestions follow:

❑ Cover sheets are important pieces of paper. Be sure they have the following information: sender's name, company, address, phone number, and fax and e-mail number. Always indicate how many pages are being sent. It's a courtesy as well as a precaution.

Another Wayne McKinnon Tip: Ask the recipient if they require a cover sheet. Home-office recipients often don't want or need one. Sticky notes can be purchased that are specifically designed for faxing.

❑ Cover sheets are also the first image that your customer has of you. Professionalism reigns in your decision as to how to compose it.

❑ Don't send any correspondence in less than 10-point font or with colored ink. They just don't transmit well.

❑ If you have documents with pictures that you send frequently, have a low-resolution copy on hand for faxing. Most high-resolution pictures appear as an all-black object. 150 dots per inch (DPI) may work well. Low-resolution high-contrast images work best.

❑ Sending faxed documents directly from your computer produces a better quality document than one sent via a low-resolution fax machine.

IN SUMMARY

I showed you how to prevent disasters before you send your message and provided invaluable guidance for all your electronic communication. Having pride in your work requires paying attention to details. Those details are important whether you're sending an 80-page report or a one-paragraph e-mail. I encouraged you to purchase a reference handbook for punctuation, spelling, and capitalization specifics not covered in this section. The same advice goes for the intricacies of e-mail. Lots of sources are available online or in books. You might consider using Wayne McKinnon's book as a reference as you participate in the continual explosion of the Web with its on-going wonders.

What's Next

In the next chapter, you will learn:

🖈 Tips for memos that get read

🖈 The basics of a business letter

🖈 The do's and don'ts of letter writing

🖈 Effective models for "good and bad" news letters

🖈 The elements of a successful sales letter

🖈 How to organize PR letters and news releases

🖈 How to write thank-you and acceptance letters

🖈 An easy format for business proposals and reports

 *Hi ho, hi ho, it's off to work we go!*

CHAPTER SIX

GET WRITING

HAVE TEMPLATES, SAVE TIME

In the previous chapters, you've been empowered, encouraged, and hopefully, educated! Chapter Six can be your reference guide for those common and not-so-common writing tasks:

- Memos
- Letters
- Reports
- Proposals

You will see templates for your everyday kinds of communication along with **examples** (sometimes written tongue in cheek). Since one of the recurring themes is **saving time**, I won't disappoint in this chapter. Developing good models for frequent topics makes good sense. Just be certain that you personalize them.

 **Dr. Julie Tip:** When asked to review a company's letter templates, I always advise that they keep them fresh by reviewing, rewriting, and/or tossing out the old ones. How often? About every four to six months.

MEMOS

Memos certainly are the most widely used form of communication within an organization. The standard requirements for memos is that they be concise and to the point, so the e-mail writing guidelines from Chapter Five apply to memos as well. Here are nine important tips that will ensure your message gets read!

1 **Make memos clear, organized, and credible.** Judgements about you will be made based on these semiformal pieces of writing.

2 **Keep memos short and sweet.** Use the one-'n-one rule: one main point in one page.

3 **Save your reader time.** Like with e-mail, the subject line which is usually just a phrase, should be as specific as possible. It functions the same way as a report title.

> I write at high speed because boredom is bad for my health. It upsets my stomach more than anything else. I also avoid green vegetables. They're grossly overrated.
>
> **Noel Coward**

4 Begin with a statement of the memo's main idea (remember Power 1?). Be direct and to the point. State the purpose in the opening sentence.

5 Position your ideas; the most important goes first, followed by the next most important.

6 Be clear about what you want the reader to do with the information in your memo. Dates, details, and deadlines all help get a timely response, if one is required.

7 Do send a memo if you want to:
• Protect your idea within the organization
• Formally state your opinion regarding a decision
• Make a request
• Confirm a decision
• Praise someone for work well done

8 *Don't* send a memo if you have *any* doubts. Pick up the phone or walk down the hall. Memos have a *very* long shelf life.

9 Open with a positive statement. Then, if you have to, present the bad news and close with a possible solution or different perspective.

LETTERS

Letters endure as probably the oldest form of business communication, whether sent by snail mail or electronically. They are written primarily to inform (with good or bad news) or to persuade. Moreover, they represent *you* and your organization. Using a basic letter format is a necessary detail in your correspondence. A quick review of the standard parts to a business letter plus a list of **do's** and **don'ts** follows.

A review: Parts of a business letter

Mr. Edward Fitzpatrick

1143 West Diamond Street

Butte, MT 00000-0000

December 31, 1999

Heading: Give the complete address of sender with no abbreviations (or have all information on letterhead). You may either spell out the name of state or use U.S. Postal Service abbreviations. The date goes directly below the heading or two to four line spaces below the letterhead.

Chris Wall

Producer

Wrangler Rhythm Records

7416 Towne Avenue

Los Angeles, CA 00000-0000

Inside address: Put the name of person to whom you are writing— first name/initial, last name—followed by the title, company name, and address on separate lines. Double-check that all are spelled correctly.

Dear Mr. Wall:

We would like to invite . . .

you will be welcome to . . .

and the rest of these . . .

on the first of the . . .

Salutation: Be careful that you address the person correctly: Mr., Ms., Dr., Superintendent, etc. A colon is generally used after the salutation, but a comma may be used if you know the person and it seems appropriate.

Beginning and Body: Be sure you have an effective opening sentence. Make that first paragraph positive and informative. (Chapter Three) You can use bullets, numbers, or lists to help your reader. Elaboration on your main point(s) occurs here with Power 2's & 3's. (Chapter Two)

Therefore, if you will . . .

so we may confirm all the . . .

make the final arrangements . . .

We would like to have . . .

as soon as it is . . .

Ending: As important as the opening sentences are, your ending (Chapter Three) lets your reader know what he/she should do next and/or create goodwill. Enclosures, attachments, forms are mentioned here as well as follow-up information.

Sincerely,

Complimentary closing: Type this two line spaces below the ending of the body. Standard expressions are *Sincerely* or *Sincerely yours*. After a relationship with reader has formed, perhaps try: *Regards, Best wishes, Best regards*, or *Cordially*. Always place a comma after this closing.

Ed Fitzpatrick

Your signature: Sign your name here. It can differ from the typed professional name that will follow your signature. Again, if you have a relationship with the recipient, perhaps sign the letter just with your first name. It's your call.

Edward Fitzpatrick

Attorney-at-Law

Full name and business title on separate lines.

EF/jp

Reference Initials: Initials of the person who wrote letter (caps) followed by initials of the person who typed letter (lower case).

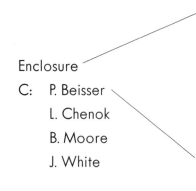

Enclosure

C: P. Beisser

L. Chenok

B. Moore

J. White

Enclosure notation: If additional material is enclosed, it can he indicated by *Enc.*, *Enclosure*, or *Enclosure*, followed by name of enclosed item, e.g., book invoices.

Copy notation: C, which stands for copy, has replaced CC. It indicates, in alphabetical order, to whom the copies have been sent.

Excuse me for not answering your letter, but I've been so busy not answering letters that I couldn't get around to not answering yours in time.

Groucho Marx

Letter Do's and Don'ts

Do:

❑ Follow the concepts and strategies presented in this book as you organize, begin, and write your letter. Be correct in every detail.

❑ Use either full block style or left justified with ragged right. These are the most common formats. All text stays to the left with no indentation at the beginning of the paragraphs. Double-space between paragraphs.

❑ Determine where to put "good" or "bad" news in your letter. It should be based on circumstances, the reader, and the purpose

❑ Call the reader by name, if appropriate.

❑ Tell the reader what you *can do.*

❑ Develop letter templates or models. Yes, it's important to consider your reader, but having a boilerplate model on hand that can be personalized will save you time, especially if you are sending out the same letter to a number of clients.

Don't:

❑ Start "bad news" letters with the bad news. Put a buffer sentence first before you disappoint or anger your reader.

❑ Manipulate your reader, put on airs, be cute, or exaggerate. He/she won't be fooled.

❑ Use canned beginnings (*Enclosed please find...*) or endings (*Call me if you're interested...*). (Chapter Three)

❑ Summarize your points at the end unless it's a long letter.

> **No one can write decently who is distrustful of the reader's intelligence or whose attitude is patronizing.**
> **E.B. White**

❑ Feel the necessity to use all the letter details presented above. Your audience and purpose will determine what you include.

LETTER TEMPLATES

This section presents usable templates or patterns for the most common types of letters.

The "good news" letter

At least half of all business letters contain a positive message. From responding to an inquiry about your product or service, to filling an order, to making an adjustment, to extending credit, to sending congratulations, they all contain information the reader is interested in receiving. These letters have a similar format:

I have made this letter longer than usual because I lack the time to make it shorter.
Blaise Pascal

Beginning: State the good, most important news enthusiastically, if that is appropriate.

Body: Give any necessary details (perhaps a sales pitch for your product).

Ending: Close with a cordial, courteous comment that creates goodwill and shows appreciation for his/her business.

This letter sends congratulations to a customer:

Dear Ms. Hart:

Congratulations on winning the Podunk lottery! We are happy to increase your advance line to $200,000. Please come into the bank to sign the documents by October 16*th*. Included with the advance line increase you will have: unlimited check writing; a free bankcard; free safe deposit box; free traveler's checks; plus we will waive the first year's annual fee on your platinum credit card.

Also, be sure to bring the certificate with you so that we can assist you in securing this advance line. We thank you for your continued business with ABC Bank and look forward to meeting all your future banking needs.

Let my receptionist know when you come in, as I would like to meet you! Or feel free to call me at 555-XXXX and set up an appointment time. I have some exciting new programs to share for special customers like you.

Sincerely,

Mallory Miles

The "bad news" letter

Letters that contain a negative message are neither pleasant to write nor to receive. The "bad news" letter may respond to a customer complaint, refuse a claim, reject an applicant, or decline an invitation. Because you are going to disappoint (maybe anger) the receiver, consideration should be extended to your reader. Put yourself in the reader's shoes as you compose this letter. Keeping goodwill while not further antagonizing him/her should be your goal:

Beginning: Start with a buffer statement. You want to create a friendly, positive tone.

Body: Include a logical explanation for your negative news. Review the facts and circumstances surrounding the decision. Details should only be included if no legal ramifications could occur. You are not always obligated to justify your "no."

> **Advice is judged by results, not by intentions.**
> **Cicero**

Ending: Close with anything positive about the situation. Offer a friendly suggestion, wish the reader future success, or present a reasonable alternative.

A familiar letter to most of us:

Dear Tony,

Thank you so much for your time and interest regarding the division manager position. You have many impressive qualities, which made the final choice a tough decision for our interview team.

Though all three of our finalists were excellent, we have hired a candidate whose qualifications best fit the position at this time.

Thank you for your interest in our company. I wish you much success in your future endeavors.

Best regards,

Christian Carter

The complaint or claims letter

This type of letter is written about a situation that needs correcting. Always treating your customer with respect no matter the circumstances. You might want to mention the service you have provided in the past and will continue to do so in the future.

Beginning: Thank the reader for notifying you. Use facts, dates, places, people, numbers, cost, etc., as appropriate.

Body: Explain clearly and logically what will be done. State sequentially why the incident occurred. Suggest alternatives if appropriate.

Ending: Close with an apology for any inconvenience or confusion that may have been caused. Maintaining good customer relations is important, so include a phone number for the reader.

This letter *rejects* a customer's claim:

Dear Mr. Matthew Burn:

Thank you for your letter concerning the replacement of your Merry Widow microwave model #12345. We have reviewed your request.

Your letter stated that after mounting it on top of your station wagon, it quit working within a week. Since Merry Widows are not designed for outdoor usage, especially during our rainy season, we cannot honor your request for a new microwave. The warranty does not extend to outdoor use. I have enclosed another copy of the instruction manual for future reference.

Please come in to our showroom soon to see our latest models—on sale! We have an excellent product line of microwaves for indoor use. If you have any further questions, please call our Customer Service Department at 555-XXXX.

Sincerely,

Angela Adams

The "customer is always right" theory seems to work best as you think about your response. Your voice—meaning the tone of the letter—is important. Be courteous and positive.

Beginning: Start with the "good news" and apologize for the error. Show that you understand.

Body: Explain logically what went wrong or what caused the problem. Also let him/her know how you plan to resolve the issue.

Ending: Show appreciation for the reader's business. Close with a pleasant, future-oriented sentence.

This letter corrects a customer's complaint

Dear Dr. Browne:

We are so sorry about your long wait at the drive-up window on May 18th. Twelve minutes is an unacceptable period of time to wait.

On that day only one teller was working the drive-up,

our staff having been temporarily reduced by the recent influenza epidemic. Our tellers are all well now, so the situation should not occur again.

In the future, if you are pressed for time, our ATM machine could be a good alternative. We would be happy to order a card for you if you don't have one. For your convenience, I have enclosed an application.

First State Bank is committed to providing top quality customer service. Please call me if you have further questions at 555-XXXX.

Sincerely,

Illiterate?
Write today for
free help!

Eamonn Edwards

Enc.

Anguished English

The sales letter

Sales letters are always about trying to *persuade* the reader to buy a product or service. The reader does not always view them with great fondness, so enthusiasm (voice) for your business must come through. The reader is only interested if your product or service directly benefits him/her. Therefore, you must get to the point quickly, directly, *and* in an interesting way.

Beginning: Hook your reader (remember Zero Power?) with an idea or an offer. You have great news: your product or service! Create interest by appealing to the desire to gain prestige or increase income; to a sense of compassion; to curiosity; or even to a wish to get something free.

Knowing your audience has never been more important! Downplay the use of *I, me, mine, my, we, our, ours,* and *us* and emphasize *you, your,* and *yours.* Depending on whether you know the recipient will determine the first sentence.

Body: Sell your product or service with convincing facts, figures, statistics, or anything that provides proof of the outstanding qualities of your product/

> **Doing business without advertising is like winking at a girl in the dark; you know what you're doing, but nobody else does.**
> **S. Britt**

service. Testimonials, endorsements, personal stories, or a limited free or reduced offer are all ways to appeal to your reader. You want to create a favorable impression of your product. Perhaps you will include brochures or pictures with your letter? Bullets or lists help the reader scan your information.

Ending: Urge your reader to do something: *call, write, send money, drive over,* or *go online.* Here you want to make it as convenient as possible for your reader to act immediately. This is a sales technique where you combine benefits with goodwill. You may—depending on purpose, audience, and circumstances—want to apply pressure by asking a question or spurring action with a deadline.

IF, you're having trouble constructing a letter, create an Idea Map! **Mapping question:** What are the major features of my company/product/services that benefit my customer/client? Once you come up with a word or phrase, put it in the middle of your Idea Map.

OR use this sentence below as a guide:

My product/service

(Describe here in detail)

has these features

(List every feature you can think of)

that benefit my customer.

(How will your product/service help your customer/client?)

Think about the advantages or strengths of your product/service by explaining its features. You need to show the reader the benefits. You also need to think about what objections your reader might have to the product.

This is a sales letter to a customer after initial contact had been made:

Dear Ms. Bethel:

It was great meeting with you this week. Did I mention that our company could provide accounting services that will increase your bottom line by $2 million annually? Our ability to manage your accounts will free up your time so that you can create an even larger client base.

Goldcoin Accounting will quickly and easily set up a system in your organization that can accomplish increased profitability and morale. First, we will streamline your accounting system. We guarantee a 20 percent (minimum!) increase in gross profits the first year. Second, we will put on a company picnic like you've never seen before. Talk about raising employee morale!

We know the needs of businesses like yours because we have firsthand experience in what it takes to manage a business. Enclosed is a client list—feel free to contact any of them. We have sent along our company brochure giving you more detailed information. I look forward to our meeting next Thursday at 10 a.m.

Sincerely,

Mark Connoy

Mark Connoy
President and CEO

Enc.

> **Writers are people who have a harder time writing than ordinary people.**
> **Thomas Mann**

The thank-you letter

This time-honored letter has gone sadly and increasingly out of style. People no longer take the time to thank others, but it remains a powerful (let alone courteous) sales and marketing tool *and* puts you above the crowd. Thanking a client for his or her account, showing appreciation to a friend for a referral, or just saying you enjoyed meeting someone spells *first rate*. You'll be remembered even more if you personalize it by adding details rather than just sending the generic form letter. The thank-you letter does not have to be long; four or five sentences will suffice. It's the thought that counts.

Beginning: Thank the reader in the first sentence for the specific act.

Body (can be part of opening paragraph): Mention why you are thanking them with specific comments.

Ending: Close with the next steps you will take (if appropriate) or a breezy goodwill statement.

PS: If you handwrite your letter, it's even classier!

Dear Jeff,

Thank you so much for giving me the opportunity to present the Business Writing That Counts! training to your employees last week. They were a wonderful group and seemed to enjoy the exercises in my book. Your department heads said that the Power Numbers system was an easy tool for them to use in organizing their year-end report.

Thank you again. I look forward to our continued relationship.

Sincerely,

Ryan Roberts

Press Releases

These documents contain information that you want to get out to the media, such as newspapers and TV or radio stations. They can be an announcement about management promotions, year-end financial reports, fund-raising efforts, or even a part of your press kit. Press releases have a definite format.

Beginning: Start with a Zero Power sentence that generates excitement, enthusiasm, and interest in your news. Don't forget to include the 5 W's (who, what, where, when, why) and the H (how) within the first paragraph. According to Candace Kovner Bel Air, a media consultant in Seattle, TV stations in major markets receive 100 press releases a day! So using words such as *first, last, new, unique, one-of-a-kind, only, different* will get yours to stand out.

Body: Include the facts with details about the organization, event, business, or product. These may be changes in management, a new acquisition or product, or a public service announcement (PSA). If the release is about your business, include any positive attributes/benefits of your product/service in order of importance. If appropriate, use a celebrity endorsement or a quote from a happy customer.

Conclusion: Get out quickly, listing any pertinent information the reader may need. If you include a sales pitch, it goes here, but create a clear and simple description.

FOR IMMEDIATE RELEASE

Contact: Ann Hill
744 Carly
Whittier, CA 00000-0000
(210) 475-1234

NEW BOOK HELPS BUSINESS WRITERS QUIT
CIRCLING THE COMPUTER!

*SOMERVILLE, NJ—***Business Writing That Counts!**
*introduces a unique approach—organizing with
numbers—to those who have to write in their work
world. This entertaining and informative book presents readers with fast and effective ways to get
started, get organized, and get writing.*

*"By using my numbering system, you can cut your
writing time in half," said Dr. Julie Miller, author of
Business Writing That Counts! *"After years of
working with people and their issues around writing, I
finally decided to write down what I'd been advis-
ing." She added that finding a way to "quit circling
the computer and get writing" is important to her
clients. "Time is always a critical factor."*

*Miller consults with individual clients as well as conducts
training seminars. She estimates that she has presented
this system to over 110,000 people nationwide.*

*Dr. Miller's book assists the full spectrum of writers.
Whether they write the occasional memo or develop*

*formal reports, **Business Writing That Counts!** pro-*
vides invaluable techniques and strategies for
completing a writing task and getting the message out.

What distinguishes this book from other business
writing books? "I've made mine very user-friendly.
Writing is intimidating enough for most people," says
Miller. "Why scare them to death? My contention is
you can break a few rules and still produce a power-
ful document."

Dr. Miller's website's offers additional writing strate-
gies (www.DrJulieMiller.com). "Yes, I wanted to have
a place where people can get help for their ordinary
as well extraordinary writing tasks."

###

Professional Reports

Documents longer than two or three pages which present information so the reader(s) can make a decision may become reports. The organizational format essentially has three major parts: Beginning, Body, and Ending.

Like the business letter, I have included all the possible components for a formal report below. The *report requirements* and *your reader* will determine what to include.

Executive Summary or Abstract

Though this is usually written last, it is placed before the introduction. Its purpose is to summarize the major points (Power 2's) of the report: the problem, the solution, the conclusions or the recommendations. The summary can be five sentences or a page but no longer. Keep the image of a *one-legged interview*—meaning, equate how long you can stand on one leg to how long you can hold your reader's attention—in back of your brain.

Bullets and lists help the reader quickly skim major points. Conclude with an explanation of how the report is organized.

 **Dr. Julie Tip:** You can use the report's table of contents or your Power Outline as an organizing guide for your abstract/summary.

Beginning

Begin with a sentence that draws your reader into the document. Include the *what, why,* and *how* in the introduction:

What: Subject/problem/issue or reason for the report

Why: Background information including purpose and scope of report

How: Methods, techniques, procedures used; define terms, where necessary; describe organization of report

 Idea: Write a strong Power 1 sentence with the number of points that will be discussed.

Body

Here's where all the details go. Courteously guide the reader through the information with headings and subheadings. Employ visual aids to make your information user-friendly:

- Headings: 2-3 per page
- White space
- Bullets or lists or numbers
- Graphics, visuals, illustrations, graphs, tables, organizational or flow charts
- Capital letters, bolded words, underlining, italics, or various fonts

Make sure that your information is logically organized. Specifics that detail the major and minor issues should be addressed here.

Conclusion

This is a very important part of your report. People tend to read the abstract or summary and then go to the report conclusion. You need to tie up all the loose ends:

- restate the purpose of the document
- draw conclusions
- make recommendations
- interpret your findings or research
- present the results of the study

Be certain that your conclusion and your introduction match. Did the report deliver what you said it would in your introduction? Whatever you wrote in the beginning of the document must be addressed in the conclusion.

Sometimes an implementation process is introduced along with a timeline including the details about cost, personnel, and time commitment.

Optional Support Material

Common sense, appropriateness, or the report requirements dictate whether you use any of the following:

- Letter of transmittal
- Title page
- Table of contents
- Appendices
- Glossary
- Bibliography
- Index
- Specific format guidelines for an individual business/organization (e.g., the U.S. government has particular format requirements for their documents as do many aerospace-related companies)

PROPOSALS

The difference between reports and proposals are in the actual words themselves. Reports *report* unemotionally about information gathered. They deliver the facts. Proposals *propose* and *persuade* a specific course of action and request action or support from the reader. The same holds true for business plans.

Proposals can be a great sales tool. They can persuade or recommend; offer a solution; present a service or product; sell a concept, idea or plan; request or seek permission or approval. The format of your proposal will again depend on its purpose, the circumstances and the ever-present *reader.* Use the specifics of the formal report template on the preceding pages as a guide. However, you may want to consider the following elements. This "think sheet" can give you a start.

Get out a piece of paper and make four columns labeled *background, problem, action,* and *plan*. Respond to each question and statement below. For **example**, your company wants to purchase a new software program. Using the sentences below, perhaps you would think about these questions: What information is pertinent? Will the new software solve productivity problems? Who needs what by when? What kind of financial commitment is involved? Who will need training?

A Proposal Think Sheet

Subject _____ Reader/s _____

Background	Problem	Action	Plan
What information is necessary so the reader can make a decision?	How can the proposal help/ correct/solve a problem?	Consider: who/how/what when	Consider: money personnel training timeline

From this Think Sheet, create a Power Outline!

Beginning: Summarize the proposed problem and your plan to solve it. Then address the benefits of your plan. How will your plan help the customer? What are the customer benefits of your solution? The level of reader knowledge will determine what or how much background information is necessary.

Body: How are your methods, materials, equipment, time, and costs most effective, efficient, and productive? What results are expected and how will you evaluate them? This can be technical as you describe the plan in detail. A logical approach—one point leading to another—helps the reader. **Examples,** illustrations, statistics, and/or details help make your case.

Ending: Summarize your key points and reemphasize the benefits. This is where you call for action and share your willingness to help.

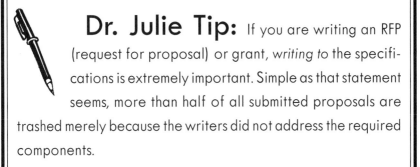

Dr. Julie Tip: If you are writing an RFP (request for proposal) or grant, *writing to* the specifications is extremely important. Simple as that statement seems, more than half of all submitted proposals are trashed merely because the writers did not address the required components.

Model Motto: These models are merely guides. Take what you need, ignore the rest.

ALL WRITE, ALREADY!

The concepts and techniques presented in this book will hold you in good stead whether you use them for report writing or electronic messaging. I encourage you to practice what you've learned so that writing becomes fast and fun! I leave you with a final checklist.

The Last Ever Writer's Checklist

Did you...

✔ **Idea Map** the topic? (Chapter One)

✔ **Power Outline** your major and minor points? (Chapter Two)

✔ Draft the document by free-writing with an edge? (Chapter Two)

✔ Write like you talk? (Chapter Three)

✔ Produce **Power 1, 2,** and **3** sentences and paragraphs? (Chapter Two)

✔ Employ **Zero Power** sentences where appropriate? (Chapter Three)

✔ Remember to count backwards as an editing device? (Chapter Two)

✔ Practice the **C.L.E.V.R.** solutions to business writing? (Chapter Four)

✔ Solicit feedback for your writing? (Chapter Three)

✔ Use correct punctuation, capitalization, and spelling? (Chapter Four)

✔ Avoid disaster before your message went out? (Chapter Five)

✔ Understand the protocol to electronic communications? (Chapter Five)

✔ Learn the basic formats of day-to-day business writing? (Chapter Six)

✔ Have fun? (Chapters One to Six)

Appendix

A Handy Reader Meter

This *Reader Meter* can help you understand your reader. Where does yours fit on this meter? Is your message focused on your reader or yourself? Think about what classification *he/she* may fall into. Depending on the purpose of the document, your approach may change.

Reader	Purpose of Message	Best Approach
Someone outside the field: w/no or limited knowledge	• General interest/ understanding of information	• SImple, short explanations and concrete examples, stories/anecdotes • Limited or no tech. lang. • Limited theory
Executive: Makes decisions & solves probs.	• Makes decisions about resources, products, services, & personnel	• Use little/no technical lang. advantages • Emphasize: Market potential of prod. alternative approaches, costs, & results
Specialist: Expert in field	• Wants/needs new information, opinions, data, techniques, theories • Analytical conclusions, results	• Little background • Factual information w/o judgment/opinions • Thorough methodology • Well-defined bibliography • Write in specialist lang.
Technician: Person who builds, maintains, services equipment/ programs	• Needs information to maintain or troubleshoot , operate, understand equipment, programs, service	• Little theory • Info. that is practical, useful in simple format practical, useful in simple format • Use a "how to" approach • Picture, graphs, charts
Operator: Carries out instructions	• Needs information to operate equipment, programs, or services	• Simple, sequential, & detailed steps • Visuals, pictures

TRANSITIONS

Reference from Chapter Three, page 79.

- **To guide the reader:** First, second, third, next, one, besides, then, before, after, finally, meanwhile, later, soon, formerly, afterward, until now, since, again, immediately, today, in the past, recently, earlier, moreover, furthermore, to begin with, above all

- **To introduce an example:** For example, for instance, to explain, specifically, to contrast, to describe, to compare, to refute, in other words, to support, to illustrate, to define

- **To add a fact, a thought, an idea:** Also, and, besides, finally, furthermore, again, moreover, next, too, as well as, in addition to, since, that is, in fact, then, similarly, additionally, another, it's true that

- **To alert reader to change in thought:** Moreover, on the contrary, however, but, nevertheless, on the other hand, the fact remains that

- **To conclude:** All in all, to conclude, in conclusion, to summarize, finally, last of all, therefore, in summary, the point is, as one can see, in short, for these reasons, to sum up, as a result, in other words, to review, I conclude that, in closing, to close

- **To compare, contrast, show cause and effect:** But, however, on the other hand, on the contrary, although, nevertheless, instead, as a result, therefore, because, consequently, yet, or, even so, similarly, likewise, still

- **To show purpose:** To this end, for this purpose, for this reason, with this objective in mind, because of

- **To show condition:** Provided, providing, on condition, in any case, subject to, whether, if, with the stipulation, with the understanding, in either case

- **To show spatial order:** Above, below, here, there, outside, inside, nearby, beyond, over, under, across

THE STEPS: FROM IDEA TO ARTICLE

1 | **Time Management Habits Idea Map**

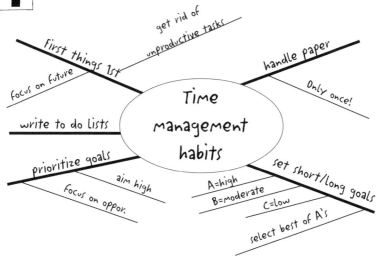

2 | **Time Management Habits Power Outline**

Power 1= time management habits
 Power 2= first things first
  Power 3= get rid of unproductive tasks
  Power 3= focus on future
 Power 2= prioritize goals
  Power 3=focus on opportunity
  Power 3=aim high
 Power 2= write to do lists
 Power 2= set short/long goals
  Power 3= A= high
  Power 3= B= moderate
  Power 3= C= low
  Power 3= select best
 Power 2=handle paper
  Power 3= only once!
Power 1= make time work

3   *Time Management Habits* **Power 1 and Power 2 sentences**

Power 1=Practicing five indispensable habits is your
        passbook to a full and rich life.
    Power 2=Do first things first.
    Power 2=Prioritizing your goals is the second habit.
    Power 2=A third habit consists of writing to do lists.
    Power 2=Set short- and long-term goals.
    Power 2=Learning how to handle the slew of paper
        that arrives each day is important.
Power 1=Make time work.

4   *Time Management Habits* **converted into Power 1 and Power 2 paragraphs**

Your passbook to a rich and full life will be assured if you practice these five indispensable time management habits.

Start by focusing on first things first. By determining the most significant work for you to accomplish, you narrow your concentration to a few activities that get results. Since not enough time is available to do everything, choose the most significant tasks and pour your energy into those.

Second, prioritize your goals. Your goals must be centered around opportunities rather than past failures. Only through ranking your objectives will you achieve focus.

A third habit consists of writing to do lists. Goal-oriented people always write things down. By doing so, goals become more than just ideas. Writing makes them real.

Fourth, setting short- and long-range goals should become an ingrained habit. This process consists of deciding what level of importance each of them has. Then organize the tasks around completing your goals.

Last, learning how to handle the slew of paper that arrives each day is imperative. Touching the same piece of paper more than once wastes an inordinate amount of time.

Making time work for you remains the most important habit you can acquire in today's extraordinarily busy world.

5 Time Management Habits converted into newsletter article with Power 1, 2, and 3 paragraphs

Your passbook to a rich and full life will be assured if you practice these five indispensable time management habits.

Start by focusing on first things first. By determining the most significant work for you to accomplish, you narrow your concentration to a few activities that get results. Since not enough time is available to do everything, choose the most significant tasks and pour your energy into those.

Repeating this daily mantra—I must do first things first—forces you to hone in on important work and eliminate those tasks that don't move you forward.

Second, prioritize your goals. They must be centered around opportunities rather than past failures. Only through ranking your objectives will you achieve focus.

Focusing on future opportunities should drive the organization. You can't change what's happened, you can only prepare for what will happen. That's where your energy and attention must be directed—outward towards success. Remember to always aim high!

A third habit consists of writing to do lists. Goal-oriented people always write things down. By doing so, goals become more than just ideas. Writing makes them real, concrete, and attainable.

Fourth, setting short- and long-range goals should become an ingrained habit. This process consists of deciding what level of importance each of them has. Then organize your tasks around completing the goals.

Label these tasks A, B, and C. A tasks always get picked as they will create results. Those tasks labeled B are placed in a file that says "pending," while the C tasks are put in a drawer that may read "when hell freezes over." Translation: No time or energy should be spent on C tasks.

Last, learning how to handle the slew of paper that arrives each day is imperative. Touching the same piece of paper more than once wastes an inordinate amount of time.

It would stagger the imagination to consider how many times you handle a piece of paper before you act on it. Force yourself to make a decision about each piece of correspondence as it crosses your desk the first time. Will you file it, toss it, or respond to it? Choose.

Anyone can acquire these five habits. Simple, tested, and proven in the real world of work, they help you accomplish more in less time, thus freeing up time for enjoyable pursuits. Making time work for you remains the most important habit you can acquire in today's extraordinarily busy world.

ADVANCED EXAMPLES

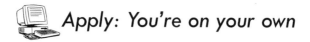 *Apply: You're on your own*

Reference from page 47.

Look at these paragraphs. Can you determine the Power 1, 2, and 3 sentences? How about the Power Numbers of the paragraphs in #3? PS: I threw in a few ringers!

#1: From a *Seattle Times* editorial

"Pardon the cynicism, but is the sport ready to rid itself of thugs and thieves? The obvious answer is no, but the iron jaws of Iron Mike could be the starting point for prying the sport away from its jackal promoters.... For boxing to survive the laughter, it must reform:

First, forbid Mike Tyson from boxing in a sanctioned bout for the rest of his life. Second, fine the promoter. A sport that draws its leading figures from penitentiaries and rewards them with millions of dollars can't be governed from within.... Third, adopt Olympic boxing standards. Tyson couldn't have gotten his teeth into Holyfield if both were wearing regulation boxing headgear."

#2: From *Harvard Business Review*

"Two stories illustrate the American way of thinking about entrepreneurship. The first related the story of the entrepreneurial hero—the plucky individual who uses energy, effort, daring and good luck to rise in the world.... The second story holds more promise."

#3: From *Food and Wine* magazine:

"Certainly there's very little controversy about the conditions that produce the world's finest wines. First, great wines come from well-situated vineyards whose microclimates are favorable to the specific types of grapes grown there.

Second, profound wines—whether they're from France, Italy, Spain, California, or Australia—are the product of conservative viticultural practices that emphasize low yields and ripe fruit.

Third, the very best wines are created by winemakers who share a noninterventionist philosophy. They permit the vineyard's terroir (soil, microclimate and the like) to express itself."

Here are the answers

#1:	Power Sentences 0 0 1 2 2 3 2 3
#2:	Power Sentences 1 2 2
#3:	Power Sentences 1 2 2 2 3
	Power Paragraphs 1 2 2

Let's add Power 4's and 5's

Expanded paragraph from *Time Management* article

A third habit consists of writing to do lists. (Power 2) Goal-oriented people always write things down. (Power 3) By doing so, goals become more than just ideas. (Power 4) Writing makes them real. (Power 5)

You Want Answers?

Power Quizzes from pages 45-47

#1   Power Sentences 1 2 3 2 3

#2   Power Sentences1 2 2 2 2 2 2

#3   Power Sentences 0 1 2 2 2 2

#4   Power Paragraphs 1 2 2 1

Pedantic Phrases rewritten from page 78

Please note/consider that

Your letter stated

Your instructions state

Whether

Say yes

Because

Next

Soon

References by Chapter

Chapter One

Buzan, Tony. *Use Both Sides of Your Brain*. New York: Dutton, 1976.

Drucker, Peter F. *The Effective Executive*. New York: Harper Row, 1966.

Funk, Charles Earle. *Heavens to Betsy! And Other Curious Sayings*. New York: Harper Row, 1955.

Hyerle, David. *Visual Tools for Constructing Knowledge*. Virginia: ASCD, 1996.

Lakekin, Alan. *How to Get Control of Your Life and Your Time*. New York: P. H. Wyden, 1973.

O'Conner, Patricia. *Words Fail Me*. New York: Harcourt Brace and Company,1999.

Rico, Gabriele. *Writing the Natural Way*. Los Angeles: Tarcher, 1983.

Wheatley, Margaret J. *Leadership and the New Science: Learning about Organization from an Orderly Universe*. San Franciso: Berrett-Koehler Publishers, Inc, 1992.

Chapter Two

Adaptation of Power Numbers system from earlier works of Socrates (469-399 BC); Hayakawa (1947) Sparks (1982); Christiansen (1979).

Lederer, Richard. *Get Thee to a Punnery*. Charleston: Wyrick and Company, 1988.

Chapter Three:

Feedback questions adapted from "Writing YOUR Natural Way," Fairfax Station: *The Type Reporter*, 1990.

Barzun, Jacques. *Simple and Direct: Rhetoric for Writers.*

Cheney, Theodore A. Rees. *Getting the Words Right: How to Revise, Edit and Rewrite.* Ohio: Writer's Digest Books, 1983

Elbow, Peter. *Writing with Power: Techniques for Mastering the Writing Process.* New York: Oxford University Press, 1981.

Lutz, William. *The New Doublespeak.* New York: Harper Collins, 1996.

Saltzman, Joel. *If You Can Talk, You Can Write.* New York: Warner Books, 1993.

Zinsser, Willliam. *On Writing Well.* New York: Harper-Perennial, 1990.

Chapter Four:

Andersen, Richard. *Writing That Works.* New York: McGraw-Hill, 1989.

Brohaugh, William. *Write Tight: How to Keep Your Prose Sharp, Focused and Concise.* Cincinnati: Writer's Digest Books, 1993.

Hamilton, Betty. *The 3 Steps to Powerful Writing.* Adrian: C & C Graphics, 1997.

Lederer, Richard. *Anguished English.* Charleston: Wyrick and Company, 1987.

Chapter Five:

Venolia, Jan. *Write Right! A Desktop Digest of Punctuation, Grammar, and Style.* Berkeley: Ten Speed Press, 1979

Chapter Six:

McKinnon, Wayne. *Wayne McKinnon's Complete Guide to E-mail.* Ontario: Ryshell Books, 1999.

Appendix:

Reader Meter adapted from Thomas Pearsall, *Audience Analysis for Technical Writing.* Glencoe Press, 1969.

ADDITIONAL SOURCE BOOKS

I find having the following books in my library to be of tremendous help. James J. Kilpatrick's *The Art of Writing* (Andrews and McMeel) is useful with his examples taken from current print. Brusaw, Alred, and Oliu's *Handbook of Technical Writing* (St. Martin's Press) is an extensive text and well worth having. Scott Edelstein's *The Writer's Book of Checklists* (Writer's Digest Books) can offer "essential information" for writers.

If you enjoy Richard Lederer's humor (*Anguished English; Get Thee to a Punnery*), you may also want to take a peek at William Safire's numerous titles on our mother tongue. And if you are really ambitious, Tom and Marilyn Ross's *The Complete Guide to Self-Publishing* is just that—complete.

INDEX

ABOUT THE AUTHOR

Dr. Julie Miller is a business writing expert. She is a consultant, author, speaker, trainer, and coach. Dr. Miller works with corporations and individuals helping improve the quality of their writing. Her primary focus is helping people reduce their writing time while still producing powerful documents.

Her book, *Business Writing That Counts!*, details a numbering system that she has taught to over 100,000 people all over the country. Dr. Miller has been a regular columnist with the *Eastside Business Journal* and written for *Washington CEO* magazine, TEC (The Executive Committee) *Diversity News* and the *Marketing Journal*.

She earned her doctorate in Adult Learning at Seattle University and holds adjunct professorships at Seattle University, Seattle Pacific University, and Western Washington University and is a visiting professor at University of Washington.

Her clients range from city governments to banks and accounting firms, from insurance companies and manufacturers to software companies. She works with executives who want to hone their writing skills and professionals who want to advance their careers.

Some of her clients include PACCAR, Inc., Microsoft, Wells Fargo Bank, Bank of America, Philip Services Corporation, Avue Techonologies, Premera-Blue Cross, City of Seattle.

Let's Keep in Touch!

If you have found your experience with *Business Writing That Counts!* valuable and would like further information about additional products and/or professional services please:

Call (425) 485-3221 or Toll free (877) DrJulie (375-8543)

Fax (425) 481-3197

E-mail Julie@DrJulieMiller.com

Write

> Dr. Julie Miller
> 14136 NE Woodinville-Duvall Road
> PMB155
> Woodinville, WA 98072-8551

Visit our website: www.DrJulieMiller.com

Order Form

Qty.	Title	Price	Total
	Business Writing That Counts!	$19.95	
	Shipping and handling Add $3.50 for orders under $20, add $4.00 for orders over $20		
	Sales tax (WA residents only, add 8.6%.)		
	Total enclosed		

Telephone orders:
Call 1-800-461-1931
Have your Visa or
Mastercard ready.

E–Mail orders:
E–mail your order request
to harapub@foxinternet.net

INTL Telephone orders:
Toll free 1-877-250-5500
Have your credit card
ready.

Fax orders:
Fax completed order form
to (425) 398-1380.

Payment: Please check one
❑ Check
❑ Visa
❑ MasterCard

Postal orders:
Send completed order
form to:
Hara Publishing
P.O. Box 19732
Seattle, WA 98109.

Name on Card: _____

Card #: _____

Expiration Date: _____

Name _____

Address _____

City _____ State_____ Zip _____

Daytime Phone (_____) _____

Quantity discounts are available. Call (425) 398-2780 for more information.

Thank you for your order!